HELL WITH THE LID OFF:
BUTTE, MONTANA

Advance Praise for
Hell With the Lid Off

"For anyone who's ever read about Butte, Montana, in its copper-mining heyday and wished they could have experienced that brawling, big-hearted time, let Horace Herbert Smith take you there. *Hell With the Lid Off* is a series of vivid snapshots from Smith, a Butte newspaperman in the 1890s when, as he writes, life there "was fast and fun." Smith died before he could publish his absorbing and entertaining memoir detailing daytime gun battles and a sermonizing standoff, the high life and labor strife, scoundrels and bullwhackers and still-breathing corpses, with a cast of real-life characters so colorful as to make fiction writers despair. Fortunately for the reader, Smith's manuscript is finally seeing print. It's a rare treat."

—Gwen Florio
Former editor, the Missoulian; author of the
Lola Wicks series of Montana mysteries

"In Montana, there's no greater task than writing something new on Butte that has not captured the imagination and research of some of the state's finest historians. Yet, every historian and writer dreams of finding a buried manuscript or trove of new material which adds color and character to the already rich history of the West's greatest mining city.

Horace H. Smith's *Hell With the Lid Off* is exactly that kind of treasure, taking the reader back to the golden age of Butte, sharing stories of Butte's thugs, miners, prostitutes, sinners and saints with details that have been almost lost.

This is truly a new addition to the first-person accounts of the historic 'Richest Hill on Earth,' and it belongs alongside the memoirs of Mary MacLane for details of Butte as it was, and it belongs next to *Copper Camp* or *The Devil Learns to Vote* for its engaging, colorful and larger-than-life stories about characters who now, thanks to Smith, have been resurrected from obscurity."

—Darrell Ehrlick
journalist, historian, editor
and Montana author

Hell With the Lid Off
Author: Horace Herbert Smith

Copyright © 2021
by New Bay Books

Editor
William Lambrecht
New Bay Books
Fairhaven, Maryland
NewBayBooks@gmail.com

Design by Suzanne Shelden
Shelden Studios
Prince Frederick, Maryland
sheldenstudios@comcast.net

Cover design by Suzanne Shelden
Interior non-captioned photo credits: page 181

A Note on Type: Cover and section heads are set in Walden Fonts' Asphaltum. The text font is ITC Bookman Standard with subheads in Walden Fonts' Civil War Type 1.

Library of Congress
Cataloging-in-Publication Data
ISBN 978-1-7348866-4-1

Printed in the United States of America
First Edition

HELL WITH THE LID OFF: BUTTE, MONTANA

A MEMOIR OF THE
"WILDEST TOWN IN THE WEST"

BY 1890S' POLICE REPORTER
HORACE HERBERT SMITH

History in the raw,
as it was lived

Above the mines where
America's mineral wealth
was dug, wealth flowed like
mud and life was fast and fun

This was Butte of the 1890s,
and for a short time thereafter
it thought it was the
greatest city in the world

And it was

CONTENTS

Preface	ix
Foreword	xi
Chapter One	1
Call of the Wild	
Chapter Two	17
Whiskey, Corruption, Gunplay	
Chapter Three	35
God v. The Devil Brings Out The Town	
Chapter Four	51
Honest Sport	
Chapter Five	69
A Newspaper Takes Root	
Chapter Six	77
The Shrewdness of Marcus Daly	
Chapter Seven	91
A Capitol Ruckus	
Chapter Eight	97
All Night Long at Theatre Comique	
Chapter Nine	109
Jail Games	
Chapter Ten	123
On the Scene of Butte's Worst Disaster	
Chapter Eleven	133
Livin' the Life of a Mining Millionaire	
Chapter Twelve	147
Close Encounters With the Barely Alive	
Chapter Thirteen	163
The Sporting Life	
Chapter Fourteen	175
A Measure of Butte's Men	
Chapter Fifteen	189
Justice With Mercy	
Addendum	193
Historical, Financial and Itemized Report	
Acknowledgements	209
Glossary	210
Photo Credits	212

PREFACE

I never knew my grandfather, but I know him through his letters and his books. He came to the United States as a young man from Canada and became a reporter in Butte, Montana, later a writer in New York City. This book is an amusing recollection of his years in Butte, when Marcus Daly ruled the roost, and vigilantes were legendary.

When my grandfather was a reporter and writer in New York, he interviewed interesting people and recounted their adventures. He became part of a salon with other writers such as Zane Grey and Sinclair Lewis. His first books, *A Captain Unafraid* and *The War Maker*, were published in 1911 and 1915. Working as a reporter during the presidencies of Theodore Roosevelt, McKinley, Harding and Coolidge, he was a member of the White House Correspondents Association.

In 1903, Samuel Langley made two attempts to fly his manned Aerodrome from a barge on the Potomac River in Aquia, Virginia. People gathered to watch, but all were disappointed. Mr. Smith covered the story for The New York Post. He was entertained at local parties, where he met and courted "Miss Annie" Fleming of Fredericksburg. They corresponded for a year, married and lived in New York where my father Horace was born. My grandmother, a devoted Virginian, labored with a box of Virginia soil placed under the delivery table.

My grandparents never divorced but lived separately; Mr. Smith suffered greatly from the separation. In 1936 he died in Fredericksburg, before he was able to publish *Hell With The Lid Off*. This book was his last, a memoir of his cub-reporter experiences in Butte.

After finding the book among his letters and documents, I decided to publish his adventures at long last.

—Melissa Smith FitzGerald
Reston, Virginia

Hell With the Lid Off

FOREWORD

I had the good fortune in 2019 to be invited for a week of writing and research in Butte, Montana, as a guest of the Mining City Writing Project. For hours at a time I took shelter from the February chill at the Butte-Silver Bow Public Archives, where archivists mine manuscripts, photographs and collections of papers like the rich ores of the surrounding hills.

Among the treasures of the Archives was an unpublished memoir by Horace Smith, who was a young police reporter at the Anaconda Standard in the 1890s, a time when Butte was a notable place on this earth. He titled it *Hell With The Lid Off.*

Horace Herbert "Bert" Smith died in 1936 while trying to finish the book and sell it to Hollywood. His granddaughter, Melissa Smith FitzGerald, who discovered the manuscript in a trunk in her Virginia home, donated it, along with his correspondence, to the Archives a month before my visit.

Ms. FitzGerald wanted this book in print, so it could stand alongside the other books her grandfather wrote during a journalism and literary career in New York. She and I thank the Archives for allowing it to be published.

The waning years of the 19th century that are the setting of Smith's book are akin to our times, with fundamentals of our daily lives transformed by the internet. Back then electricity had just arrived—and telephones!—along with an array of machines and devices, all needing copper. No place on earth produced more of the pliable yet strong, ready-for-wire red element than Butte, known as the Richest Hill on Earth.

Twenty-one year-old Horace Herbert Smith, who went by Bert, plugged into Butte in 1891 as the city was carving its special place in American history. As the late writer Edwin Dobb, a Butte native son, put it: "Like Concord, Gettysburg and Wounded Knee, Butte is one of the places America came from."

During Smith's seven years in Montana, Butte was a major city of the American West, a cauldron of riches and excess that brewed up in the three decades since gold and silver were discovered in surrounding hills. Old Vigilantes who "tamed" the region watched Copper Kings grow fabulously wealthy, political cronyism run rampant and labor union leaders brace for the coming fight with ruthless corporations.

"The black heart of Montana" was how Joseph Kinsey Howard, a Montana newspaperman and author writing in the 1940s, described Butte. He likely referred to all that had gone on in Butte and the mining mess to be reckoned with.

Fine writers bred in Montana and newly arrived have chronicled Butte's sizzling history, and that exploration continues. Butte was the inspiration for Dashiell Hammett's novel *Red Harvest* in 1929, a decade after he'd visited Montana as a Pinkerton operative on behalf of the Anaconda Company.

Smith, with his reporter's sense and access to Butte's players on all sides of the law, lends detail and perspective to well-told stories. Among them is his coverage of Butte's Great Disaster of 1895, when he escaped death amid carnage as some dozens of people died in dynamite warehouse explosions.

Often Smith is a main character in his tales. Two gambling mainstays—Billy Fay, a disfigured killer lightning quick with six-shooters in either hand, and loathsome morphine addict Frank Dougherty—both publicly declared plans to shoot him. Smith, packing himself, survived to write more about the duo.

When an atheist made a curious bet with a Presbyterian minister, Smith set the stage and held the money. A thousand people turned out at a ramshackle church for the moment of truth and the emergence of a star.

Smith tells tales of scoundrels, scandalmongers and prizefighters, and the prostitute who fooled a San Francisco detective, but he also divulges their secrets.

"The liveliest camp on earth," Smith writes of Butte. "Easterners charged it with being not only the wickedest town in the United States but with the added offense of boasting of that fact. "

Hell With the Lid Off

Smith's memoir recalls a lively era of newspapers, newly energized by the invention of the linotype machine. Back in New York, where Smith was soon to carry forward his career, Joseph Pulitzer and William Randolph Hearst—whose fortune sprung from gold mines—waged a yellow journalism war that emboldened the industry to take risks in what they served up to readers.

In Butte and nearby Anaconda, three dailies and nine weeklies hummed along. The shrewd Marcus Daly had found the massive copper vein that made him a megarich man able to satisfy any worldly desire, whether owning the fastest thoroughbreds in America, or the Standard, a newspaper born thanks to a horse, as Smith tells it. He brought in editors from New York (Smith, a Canadian by birth, hired away from the Cedar Rapids Gazette) and the paper grew steadily into a political power, circulating in San Francisco, Denver, Salt Lake City and even Chicago.

Daly was Smith's boss and he all but deifies him, while trashing other Montana millionaires who left Montana for Manhattan with what they'd earned and learned.

In his Montana memoir, Smith evidences a method he would hone in New York: earning trust of adventuresome characters and lawmen, then making as-told-to stories into books. He had an eye for newsworthy people and knew how to cultivate them for a story. Most tilted their heads upward to look at him; he stood six-foot-three and filled out into a large man, a later photo shows.

Smith comes off as something of a rascal. He describes indoor shooting sprees with law enforcement pals. He packed his own six-shooter—one with notches denoting kills—a gift from police. He was jailed once for stinting on alimony to a bride he'd brought from Iowa. His typewriter settled scores. In a story Smith wrote in February, 1895, he devoted more than three columns of his broadsheet newspaper exposing the minister's plagiarism with the soaring prose from a famed man of the cloth. What the local minister added to the pilfered texts wouldn't "satisfy the brains of a cat," he wrote in the Standard.

Smith moved to the rival Butte Miner in 1897 first as a reporter and then as an editor. A year later, he departed Montana for other posts and journalism adventures.

In the spring of 1902, by then managing editor of the Cincinnati Post, Smith set out for Martinique to cover the eruptions of Mount Pelee, a famed blow-out in our hemisphere that killed hundreds. He was the only newspaper reporter aboard the French warship *Tage*, gaining passage from New Orleans. His adventure evolved after the Post's owners, the Scripps-McRae League of Newspapers, contributed $300 to a relief fund. Smith, after racing to Louisiana on a special train to catch the vessel's departure, delivered the money in gold.

He nearly became a victim himself when Mount Pelee erupted again soon after he arrived, sending Smith, a photographer and their entourage on a desperate flight back down the mountain.

HIS HOT RACE FOR LIFE, read the headline in the Anaconda Standard, which picked up Smith's account of the drama.

His old pals at the Standard had teasing fun with a sub-head: The Terror of the Vomit of Fire, Smoke and Molten Matter Caused a Run for Your Whiskers, and Bert Could Run. Another story ran under the headline: SMITH RESCUES SEVEN: Famous Volcano Correspondent Discovers Them in Time.

Later in New York, Smith turned to writing books. In *Captain Unafraid: The Strange Adventures of Dynamite Johnny O'Brien*, (1911), Smith wrote in the first-person voice of Capt. George B. Boynton, a Civil War hero and seafaring revolutionist in Latin America. Boynton, a New Yorker of breeding and elan, had captured the city's imagination for decades. In one long-running saga, he'd played a significant role helping Cubans gain their independence from Spain.

Smith was still interviewing Boynton days before he died, getting down his stories of outwitting the Spanish, federal agencies and Pinkerton detectives in the Atlantic and Caribbean as they chased ships he captained laden with arms and ammo. A New York Times writer likened Smith's book to Alexandre Dumas' *The d'Artagnan Romances*, based on the life of the 17th century musketeer.

Smith's *Crooks of the Waldorf* (1930) chronicles the sleuthing of a hotel detective who snares schemers and thieves in New York's 1920s' sumptuous hotel scene. The London-born house dick, who learned tricks at Scotland Yard, was so crafty that New York City police mined his expertise.

Smith drew on his Montana years as editor of another book, *Roosevelt in the Rough* (1931). Jack Willis, Roosevelt's Western guide and hunting confidant, was title author in the book Smith assembled. Spiced with yarns from T.R.'s campfire conversations, the book triggered controversy when Roosevelt's son, Kermit, backed out of writing the introduction.

Teddy Roosevelt had been dead a decade. But his family was unwilling to endorse an account of the president at a rowdy dinner with buckets of champagne and near-gunplay, after which he'd engaged in decidedly un-presidential behavior atop a horse-drawn cab on a flying joyride.

Smith told the New York Times he had affidavits to back it all up. The mystery—and Smith's source—may be revealed here with publication of this manuscript. He writes herein about "Fat Jack" Jones, a legendary, rail-thin, tophat-adorned hack driver who prominent visitors to Butte sought out because of his reputation. Smith relates that Roosevelt called for Fat Jack after the raucous party, a scene implying that the president and party of three were feeling no pain.

"It was a wonderful night and wonderful air, which Roosevelt declared would 'put new life in an Egyptian mummy'," Smith writes.

"The president kept yelling 'faster, faster, Jack' until the horses were galloping madly over the flat. With the carriage swaying from side to side, in a way well calculated to throw him out on his head, he insisted on standing up from time to time and roaring out: 'Yippee, this is the life! By Godfrey, this air is great. But speed 'em up a little, Jack'. His companions were alarmed by the danger of a catastrophe but Roosevelt maintained his balance like a sailor in a seaway. And he kept the horses running until his train left."

Praising *Roosevelt in the Rough*, a prominent reviewer of the day said it ought to be placed with the body of literature associated with the 26th president.

Smith was working on *Hell With The Lid Off* when he died suddenly, of a coronary occlusion, on Jan. 25, 1936. He was 67. Now: It wasn't finished, and because of ill health he had been unable to travel to Montana to authenticate everything in his memoir.

But major episodes he described did indeed occur, and virtually everyone he named existed.

Smith's title, *Hell With The Lid Off*, has been deployed in various forms since James Parton, writing in The Atlantic Monthly in 1868, assembled words to describe the night-time glow of Pittsburgh. It's been adopted for a hip-hop album and for a book about the National Football League.

The words came to Smith as he gazed down from the fifth floor of a new Butte club, one with an elevator, at an array of saloons and bawdy houses. In the background that night, smelters belched thick yellow smoke and illuminated the sky with their red glare.

"I was a tenderfoot who had been intently studying the animated scene," he writes. "I sententiously unburdened myself of the verdict that this town certainly looks like hell with the lid off."

With this book, New Bay Books returns his title to him.

—William Lambrecht
New Bay Books

P.S. For the occasional unfamiliar term, see the Glossary.

What Nerve Berries have done for others they will do for you.

15TH DAY.

30TH DAY.

1ST DAY.

VIGOR OF MEN

Easily, Quickly and Permanently Restored.

A positive cure for all Weaknesses, Nervousness, Debility, and all their train of evils resulting from early errors and later excesses; the result of overwork, sickness, worry, etc. Develops and gives **tone** and **strength** to the **sexual organs**. Stops **unnatural losses** or **nightly emissions** caused by **youthful errors** or excessive use of **tobacco, opium** and **liquor,** which lead to **consumption** and **insanity.** Their use shows immediate improvement. Insist on having the genuine **NERVE BERRIES.** Convenient to carry in vest pocket. Price $1.00 a box, 6 boxes, one ful. treatment, $5.00. Guaranteed **to cure any case.** If not kept by your druggist we will send them by mail, upon receipt of price, in plain wrapper. Pamphlet free.

For Sale in Anaconda by the Smith Drug Co and in Butte by E. E. Gallogly & Co.

OPIUM OR MORPHINE HABIT
PAINLESSLY & PERMANENTLY CURED

DR. S. B. COLLINS'

CHAPTER 1
CALL OF THE WILD

A teetotaling tenderfoot with a typewriter

'Saloon keepers and gambling house proprietors were the only men with any value as sources of news'

It was in the winter of 1891 that I landed in Butte. I was always strong for the freedom of the frontier, as a result of a double strain of pioneer blood inherited from entirely unrelated grandparents who shook the dust of the East from their clothes and fared forth to settle in what was then the Far West, with only Indians for neighbors.

The call that would not be denied came through Jim Miller, a newspaper man fresh from Butte, with the smell of sulphur still in his clothes. Our trails crossed in Cedar Rapids, Iowa, just after I had graduated from the cub reporter class. Jim had left Butte only a few weeks before because of the natural objections to it as a place of residence by the young lady he had recently married. She had found there none of the advantages to which she had been accustomed in the East, but only disadvantages and drawbacks galore, so they packed up their things and wended their way "back to the States."

Jim's first-hand stories of life in a mining camp left nothing to be desired but the matter of getting there. At his suggestion I wrote W.W. "Wally" Walsworth, manager of the Butte office of the Anaconda Standard, giving him the name and address of a young and ambitious reporter who was possessed with a great desire to breathe the thin and free air on the crest of the Rockies. Wally, as everybody knew him, replied that there would be an opening on his staff by the time I got there, that my letter satisfied him I could write. He said he would take a chance on my ability to rustle news if I could take a chance on having to walk back East.

My resignation was in the hands of the publisher of the Cedar Rapids Gazette 10 minutes after I received this letter and in a little more than two weeks I was on my happy way West.

On my arrival Wally took me out on a personally conducted tour of the camp to make me acquainted with its leading citizens. Almost without exception they were saloon keepers and gambling house proprietors. They were the only men with any value as sources of news. Wally was a hail-fellow-well-met at every port of call, and as we faced the bar, which we were able to do only after forcing our way through a crowd in most cases, a bottle of whiskey was promptly set up in front of us, with two glasses. When I called for ginger ale the barkeeps assumed that I wanted it as a chaser, to which purpose its use was restricted, and they displayed amazement when I explained that that was all I wanted to drink.

The only soft drink in the camp, I discovered, was a concoction known as "ironwater," which was something like sarsaparilla. The old-timers had given it that name, derisively no doubt, on account of its softness and because it was said to be bad for the system. So, switching to accommodate the barkeeps, who were very busy, and prevent any delay in their work, I switched my libations and brazenly called for ironwater, with all the artlessness of the tenderfoot. Many black looks were handed to me, and there would have been worse if Wally had not been my guardian angel, though I did not realize that at the time.

As we went down the line Wally's manner changed from warm cordiality to something like aloofness, but I thought perhaps that was because he did not carry his liquor well —though any such supposition would have been a great mistake, as I soon learned. At about the tenth drink place we met Jim Lynch, who was the biggest of the town's aldermen and about the most important member of the government. Jim was behind the bar, giving his hired men a helping hand in the rush and wearing the room white apron that went with the job. He greeted us as old friends, allowed that the drinks were on the house and set out the bottle and glasses.

When I called for ironwater the smile left his face and he gave me a hard look, in which there was a mixture of incredulity. At first he would not believe his ears, and when I repeated the order his stare became stony. But all he said was: "Well I'll be damned!"

That set Wally off. He turned and faced me, looked me up and down slowly, and then inquired, incisively: "For God's sake, don't you ever drink?"

"No."

"Well," after a long pause, and with a look of surprise and disgust which had made no effort to hide, "you are going to do damned well here."

However, I did well enough to remain seven years, despite the attempts of a few bad men, who resented intrusion into their personal affairs—or affairs which they regarded as strictly personal, even though they were not—to shorten either my stay or my days, and came away in excellent health and on my own motion. Wally was a bit chilly and offish for a time but it was not a great while until he became convinced that it really was a good thing to have one member of his staff who stayed sober. So he not only forgave my abstinence from alcohol but actually endorsed it. It allowed him greater freedom of action and permitted longer sluff games, free from interruption, in the back room of Ernie Lange's saloon, which was the newspaper hangout and was conveniently situated next door to our office.

I was given the police run, including mining accidents and coroner's cases, and general charge of sporting events. That was really quite a chore in those days and it probably was just as well that I left John Barleycorn alone.

As I did not drink or play faro or stud poker—nor do I yet know how, though I have watched men playing hundreds of times—the saloon keepers and gambling house proprietors looked me over with cold and fishy eyes for quite some time. But when they finally became convinced that I was perfectly content to let every man run his own game as he gosh-danged pleased so long as he gave me the same privilege, and that I had no fool notions of trying to introduce any Eastern ways of reform ideas into the camp, we became good friends. But for a long while, as the only man in the camp who frequented the saloons yet never took a drink I was looked on as something of a curiosity and regarded with a good deal of wonderment.

THE LAST OF THE "BAD" CAMPS OF THE WEST

Butte was then wide open, in all the term implies, and probably always will be, for that matter, though in lesser degree. Physically, it was altogether repulsive, for it did not contain a tree or flower or blade of grass, as a result of the smoke from heap roasting, which was going strong, on the flat south of town. But it was alive in every fiber of its being. Gambling houses were on Main Street, in the heart of the camp, and saloons were everywhere. Both were open day and night, and every day, though they did most of their business at night. They were licensed and lawful and recognized as perfectly proper enterprises with highly laudable purposes. Everybody gambled and everybody drank and everybody enjoyed life to the full.

Butte had only 40,000 people living within its restricted limits but there were nearly as many more in Walkerville,

Hell With the Lid Off

Centerville and Meaderville, which were built right up to it and were a part of the city in everything except government and taxes. The male population was equal to that of an Eastern city of three or four times its size. The camp's inhabitants came from all parts of the world. The miners were Irishmen, Cornish men, who were known as "Cousin Jacks," and Welshmen. The men employed in the smelters were largely Italians, with the addition of a heterogeneous mess from southern and middle Europe who were known collectively as "Bohunks" to avoid a more definite classification that would have been difficult in many cases.

With the payrolls of the big companies—the Anaconda, the Boston & Montana and the Butte & Boston—running well of $1,000,000 a month and with independent companies and individuals operating at a profit, Butte had plenty of money. And it spent it in streams and rivers. The miners worked in eight hour shifts so there was always approximately one-third of the male population engaged in its favorite occupation.

The days were comparatively quiet and orderly, but when night fell the whole scene was transformed. Men crowded into the gambling houses and saloons, and around them, in such numbers that if one was in a hurry he was obliged to walk in the streets, which were free of all modern improvements and, in rainy weather, run the risk of being swallowed up in a mudhole.

Concert halls, vaudeville theaters and hurdy-gurdies sprang into life, and gambling houses and saloons largely increased their forces, and the camp became a wild jumble of bucking faro, drinking, dancing and dumping silver on the stages of the theaters, to the accompaniment of uproarious goings on. And the racket continued until daylight, by which time everybody was worn out.

The last of the "bad" camps of the West, Butte held title to the claim for years after all of the others had become bywords of propriety. It had as many killings to its credit, or discredit, as you prefer, as any of them and if it was less well known to fame that was partly because it was farther away from the East and partly because of its location. Situated more than a mile in the air on the main range of the Rockies, within gunshot of the continental divide, it stood at the head of a little valley perhaps 20 miles long by half as wide, which was entirely surrounded by high mountains. The rest of the world was somewhere over the hills; but Butte was on the inside, and it was quite well satisfied with what it saw. As the old-timers put it when some self-sufficient newcomers sought to introduce some new-fangled idea of government: "Butte was here first." In other words, if the stranger didn't like the way things were run he could move on, without the slightest feeling in the matter.

Death might be just around the corner, but for the man who attended to his own business, and took no part in strictly local affairs that were likely to end in trouble, Butte was as safe as any place in the country. But it was a most unhealthy location for the man who was looking for trouble or one who had a penchant for poking his nose into places where it did not belong. For one of the great charms of the camp was its habit of attending to its own affairs. And it did that mighty well all things considered. Calls for assistance from the outside were responded to generously, but there was never a time when Butte extended its hand across the mountains looking for a handout.

LAW OF THE VIGILANTE

For Butte was different from every other city in the country in that it was sufficient to itself and a law unto itself. It made its own regulations, when they were needed, and all laws that ran to the contrary, whether state or federal, were simply ignored. And nothing was ever done about it. Public opinion was supreme. This was directly attributable to the teachings and influence of the old Vigilantes, many of whom were still living when I was in the camp.

They were natural warriors, those noble old trail-blazers; Among them were men who whacked bulls pulling wagon trains across the plains, with free gold and a free country at

Hell With the Lid Off

the end of the long and dangerous trek. And the Argonauts who took $100,000,000, and more, in yellow dust and nuggets out of Alder Gulch, where Virginia City was established, with its neighboring camps of Nevada City, Junction, Summit, Pine Grove, Highland and Fairweather, the name of the old buckaroo who made the original discovery; in Last Chance Gulch, where Helena now stands; and in the rich placer diggings of Silver Bow Creek, where the first cabins were built. With the petering out of the gold, first silver and then copper were uncovered in the hills a mile North of the little stream and the camp became a boomtown, taking its name from the larger of two hills that rose west of Missoula Gulch, close by, which also produced some gold.

In the meantime there was a little hiatus, during which the pioneers admitted to themselves that the camp had seen its best days. All of them were trying to sell lots, which they had accumulated in one way or another. Often it was possible only when the buyer was drunk. About that time H.A. D'Acheul blew into the camp, with a pocketful of money, a great desire for stud poker and an unquenchable thirst. He was immediately seized on and made much of. At poker games in McGovern's saloon, when he had reached the right stage of inebriation, he bought many choice lots for a birdlike song. Then silver was found, then copper, D'Acheul quit drinking and playing poker, for big stakes, and became wealthy. But no one envied him his luck, for Butte was never jealous of any person or anything.

The Vigilantes, who used to say that they "came into the country when the Big Butte was a hole in the ground," were intense in their likes and dislikes. They adhered religiously to the old maxim of the West that their friends could do no wrong and their enemies could do no right. They divided mankind into two classes, with a clearly defined line between them. If a man's word was good, always, he was respected and treated as a brother, without any regard at all to the extent of his worldly possessions. Such a man never wanted for friends nor for help if he needed it. But if a man's word was not good, at all times and under all conditions, he was despised and rejected, no matter how much money he had. Name or family or fortune counted for nothing. It was their hatred of dishonesty and their suffering from it that brought about the formation of the Vigilantes, in the early days of Alder Gulch.

If the thieves had operated separately there would have been no organized opposition to them, for there was not one among the bullwhackers who would not have much preferred to conduct his own warfare and "kill his own snakes." But the highwaymen had a powerful and extensive organization, headed by Sheriff Henry Plummer, who had been elected sheriff despite being a convicted killer and an outlaw. His deputies, with the exception of one honest man whom Plummer soon killed, were bandits. His gang was composed of the most brutal desperadoes in the Northwest, who poured into the new camp as soon as the gold began to pour out of it. They were robbing and killing prosperous miners on every hand. There were between 110 and 235 robberies and murders up to the fall of 1863, and practically all of them were committed for no other reason than to prevent identification by their victims.

Only a band of brave men with determined spirits could expect to cope with lawlessness that was so well organized and so shrewdly directed. Out of this need grew the Vigilance Committee of deathless fame. It had its nucleus among the members of a powerful secret order who were bound together by the obligations of their brotherhood. They added to their number by selecting other honest men, who had never laid a stone but who could be trusted not to betray their secrets. They quietly organized, by electing W.F. Sanders, afterward United States Senator from Montana, prosecuting attorney; Paris S. Pfouts, president; and Captain James Williams, executive officer; and proceeded to clean things up in Alder Gulch.

The robberies and murders were committed in secret but the hangings were in public, for everyone to see. Every man who was taken in charge by the Vigilantes was given a fair and public trial, though his guilt had been well established before he was taken into custody. In spite of that he was given a chance to prove his innocence, but none ever did. There was no quibbling; it was a question only of facts. With a verdict of guilty, the prisoner was given time to say a prayer or write a letter home before he was strung up, kicking. That was the limit of delay permitted in the execution of the sentence.

Sheriff Plummer begged like a dog for his life, when his time came, but many of his gang went out bravely and some of them confessed. When the highwaymen became panic stricken, toward the close of the lynching parties, and took to the hills, little bands of Vigilantes were assigned to follow them and execute the sentence. Some of them had to track their quarry for days, but when they caught him he was promptly hanged to the nearest tree. Somewhere between 30 and 40 of the wretches were disposed of at the end of a rope.

From a hotbed of lawlessness, Virginia City, 50 miles or so to the southeast of Butte, became as peaceful and law abiding a community as could be found the world over. Honesty was so firmly established that a man could go to sleep with a fortune under his pillow in the most remote part of the diggings in the sure and certain knowledge that he would not be disturbed. For the Law of the Vigilante was supreme and there was no one left to question it.

PASSIONATELY IN LOVE WITH FREEDOM

Every man in that famous organization was an individualist to his fingertips, but they stuck together with a tenacity that nothing could shake long after the need for their activities had disappeared. They had lived long under the stars, in a covered wagon at night or in the open under a blanket, with a pick and shovel on one side of them and a rife or six-shooter on the other, and they chafed under the conventions of civilization. It was the restrictions on personal liberty imposed by mankind in the mass that had driven them from their Eastern homes and they were passionately in love with the freedom they had found in the far country. So it was that every effort to introduce the customs that prevailed "back in the States," which was the terse description of all the country East of the "Big Muddy," as they knew the Missouri River, was fought by the old-timers at every step—"at every mark in the road," as they phrased it.

They resented the attempts of tenderfeet, who, in their sight, were as unfit to associate with real Westerners as one of those unspeakable persons who smoked cigarettes, to fasten fixed and formal government on the new country they had opened up and made safe for men of much less courage but greater avarice. They protested vigorously when the price of the cheapest liquor was reduced from "two bits" to a "bit" a drink, or two for a quarter. All amounts less than a dollar were designated in "bits;" a quarter was "two bits," 50 cents was "four bits," and 75 cents was "six bits." 15 cents was a "long bit" and 10 cents was a "short bit."

A single drink, which was rarely called for, cost 15 cents; there were no pennies in Butte until long after I left. Joe Whatley, who for years ran the best restaurant in the camp, brought two or three hundred back with him from his annual trip East and distributed them among his friends as souvenirs. The introduction of the first 99-cent sales by a new store in the middle nineties caused an uproar that threatened to end in a boycott of the establishment. The trail-blazers and all of their friends refused to allow their women folk to accept pennies and summarily ordered them to stay away from the new store entirely if it insisted on handing out the despised copper coins. The terrified merchant compromised by giving postage stamps in small change instead of pennies, and this practice continued, perforce, for several years. Gold and silver were the only mediums of exchange. No bank would ever hand out currency unless it was called for by some new arrival in the camp.

Hell With the Lid Off

The fact that a drink of any kind of liquor could be bought for a "bit" was gall and wormwood to the bullwhackers. All of their sensibilities were outraged and they flocked en masse to the one saloon—run by Jim McGovern, who had settled in the camp in the early days—which maintained the minimum price of "two bits" a drink for ordinary liquor and "four bits" for better stuff. There they foregathered to talk over the old days and call down curses on the heads of the darned tenderfeet.

They growled loudly and protested profanely when, in the middle nineties, the telephone company felt called upon to publish requests in the newspapers in advance of the Fourth of July, Christmas and New Year's Day, politely asking celebrants to discharge their firearms into the ground instead of in the air, on account of the promiscuous cutting of wires by hilarious bullets. In those days the saloons were crowded on the eve of every important holiday—and on every other night, for that matter, though there was little shooting for fun at other times. At intervals that might be quite short and were never long, all of the men at the bar would swim out onto the sidewalk and empty their guns in the air, in honor of whatever event was being observed. And this would be kept up all night, all over town, greatly to the consternation of guests from the East in adjoining hotels, some of whom occasionally developed the need for medical attention.

Telephone and telegraph wires were cut in many places by these fancy fusillades and both services were crippled for days. But in the minds of the old trail-blazers that was a trifling detail that was not worth talking about. The telephone was considerable of a nuisance, anyway, they argued, and telegrams could wait. They had waited for weeks and months for messages from the East when they first came into the Territory, yet they managed to get along nicely. To them it was an affront and an invasion of his personal rights for any man to be requested, even with great deference, to shoot in any particular direction.

In its booming days, which extended close up to the final days of the last century, Butte was wholly untrammeled, perfectly natural in its always colorful and variegated activities and its enjoyment of life, and open and above-board in all it did. Everything was exposed in the raw, with not trimmings or decorations of any sort. If people liked things that way, Butte suited them down to the ground; if they didn't, it made no difference. Its men were virile if not violently virtuous and they were frank and honest and clean and decent in the big things of life.

One of their outstanding traits was their great respect for woman. The feminine population was small in those days and a considerable part of it was confined to the restricted part of the camp that was known as the "Bad Lands." But neither residence nor occupation made any difference when a woman appeared in public. In the place she called home she might be a plaything for any man who cared to pay the price, but when she appeared on the street, properly garbed and away from her own bailiwick, she became a lady. A crowd of men loafing on the sidewalk would make way for her as quickly as for the wife of a mine superintendent or shift-boss and show her the same tribute of silent respect as she passed.

And, after the manner of the old Argonauts, the men of Butte minded their own business. That was one of the rules of the camp which no old-timer ever violated and new-timers violated only once. A man was not supposed to sit in at any game, or deal himself a hand in argument unless had first bought chips, either literally or figuratively. If he had bought chips he was assumed to know the rules of the game and govern himself accordingly. If he failed to do that he was likely to encounter a run of very hard luck.

If you happened to be walking along the street and ran into a shooting scrape, you were supposed to keep right on going, instead of stopping to take observations. You might run, if you liked, thereby proving yourself a rank tenderfoot, unless you were actually in danger from flying lead, but you were required to keep moving. If you knew one of both of

Hell With the Lid Off

the participants well enough to take a personal interest in the affair you had the privilege of standing aside until the dispute had been settled.

When two men chanced to be seized at the same moment with an uncontrollable ambition to make a little business for the coroner, and began shooting at each other, the rules of the game provided that they must be given all of the room they needed and there must be no interference, from friend or foe or stranger. There was never anything approaching a panic at ordinary little encounters of this kind, unless partisans of the two belligerents felt called upon to take a hand in the fracas, with the idea of making more work for the undertaker. In such cases there was likely to be a bit of a stampede for whatever doors were handy, even by men who had grown accustomed to trials of marksmanship in public places. But, as a rule, the bystanders simply stepped or slid out of the line of fire and then turned around to watch developments, with trained and critical eyes. With such an expert audience, personal pride was added to enmity, and the impromptu battle that did not end in a fatality was rare.

When the establishment of a police system came up the bullwhackers arose in their might and insisted that the man at the head of it be given the title of city marshal. That had been the title of the law officer of the camp in the early days and they declared that what was good enough for him was good enough for anybody. The chief of police was a subordinate official and was on duty during the night. As in the case of Chet Small, a man might be a professional gambler under one city administration and city marshal under the next one, and then return to his former occupation. Chet was an efficient head of the police department, at that, as city marshals went in those days. He was one of the old-time gamblers and his honesty was above question.

The policemen wore no uniforms until the late nineties and carried no clubs, their only insignia of office being a star, which practically all of them wore under their coats. They were armed with heavy .45 caliber Colts, and when force was necessary in making an arrest—or when as sometimes happened, the office had a personal grudge against the man he was taking into custody—the cop used the barrel of his gun as a club, putting his finger back of the trigger to prevent any wild shots. Once in a while this precaution would be neglected or a finger would slip. One night a man was shot in the leg by the accidental discharge of the gun of an officer who found him making himself obnoxious in the Bad Lands. It was only a flesh wound, but he was dead when they got him to the police station. He was a rancher from the eastern part of the state and unused to the ways of the camp and it was assumed that he died from fright. It didn't make much difference anyway, so far as public opinion was concerned.

The force was composed of men who had worked in the mines or smelters and they had many friends. They would go into a saloon and take a drink whenever they were invited, which was often enough, and it required something out of the ordinary to force them to make an arrest. More than three-quarters of them were on the night shift, which was the period of greatest activity. They enjoyed a good fight as much as anyone and would watch a lively battle with approving interest. If it assumed a seriously threatening aspect they were likely to intervene, but probably only to the extent of shooing the fighters away in opposite directions. As a matter of fact, the chief duty of the police was to keep the crowds moving and to see that tenderfeet behaved themselves and were not unduly abused.

The camp had so many attractions for the sportively inclined that it drew bad men from all over the West. They were of all kinds and all classes. Most of them were really dangerous only when they were full of dope. Others, with naturally dour dispositions, became dangerous after a long run of bad luck at the faro tables. A few of them were naturally mean and vicious. They generally found what they were looking for among their own kind, and, sooner or later, took their last ride on the "wagon with the feather dusters on it," which was the camp's name for a hearse.

Every faro table had a gun in the right hand drawer, which was exposed every time it was opened to take out gold or silver or chips, but it was not often called into service. Any man could carry a gun who wanted to, but there were few who went armed all of the time. The man who habitually packed a revolver was looked on as genuinely bad, and if he carried it tucked in the waistband of his trousers he was considered "plain poison," and given a wide berth by everybody who was not looking for a fight. "Shooting out the lights" in a saloon or resort was a playful pastime that was occasionally indulged in but individual injury in incidents of that kind was rare.

Butte was that kind of a camp when I invaded it, and the life of a police reporter during the years when it was at its best and liveliest was filled with activity and diversion.

CHAPTER 2
WHISKEY, CORRUPTION AND GUNPLAY

"Plain poison" Billy Fay and no-good Frank Dougherty declare I'm dead

"Dougherty was a crooked gambler of the tinhorn type and a morphine fiend, a man-killer when he was full of dope and a sneaking coward without it"

However much the dispensers of the camp's favorite commodity were disturbed by my abstemiousness, I cheered them up considerably when I dropped from the water wagon with a jolt that turned in fire alarms from three different sections of town. That was after I had been in the camp nearly three years, which continued term of residence entitled me to be classed as a young old-timer.

Always fast in everything it did, Butte began the celebration of its holidays on the day before, to be sure it would miss nothing. On the afternoon of one July 3rd I ran afoul of a party of distinguished drinkers who were setting out to observe the Glorious Fourth in due and ancient form. John Maguire, manager of the "Opera House" that bore his name—the best known theatrical man in the Northwest and famous in the profession as "sixty-and-forty John" on account of his percentage rule, which troupers acceded to only because they needed the money and were sure of packed houses. J. M. Quinn, editor of the Miner, which was owned by W.A Clark and who, therefore, was fair

Hell With the Lid Off

game in any contest, and Harry Aleshire, secretary of the street railway company, each of whom prided himself on his prowess at the bar, were the chief conspirators, though it was quite a large party.

Invited, and urged to have a drink, I called for the inevitable ironwater. They sneered at that, good-naturedly, and then Quinn suggested that I was "afraid" to drink anything stronger. He was supported in that view to an extent which made it obligatory on me, as I saw it, to announce that if they felt that way about it, it would be necessary for me to put them all to bed, just to show them that they had not come honestly by their reputations. So, first taking the precaution to serve notice on Wally that I was off duty until he heard from me further, in which decision on being advised of the reason for it, he gave enthusiastic encouragement, I joined the wine-bibbers.

As it was something in the nature of a public celebration, we felt that we should not confine our purchases to one place nor play any favorites. So we circled the business district and stopped at every respectable saloon along the way to take on more wine. Between stops those of the party who carried hardware emptied it in the air, and there were loud cheers every time a broken wire came down, twisting. Taken by and large, the evening and night were very large and chockablock with song—or what passed for song, and as none of the barkeeps objected to it there were some in the party who considered it good.

Along about sunup, our supply of ammunition was exhausted and we went on a hunt for fireworks. Fortune was kind by rewarding our search with an old cannon, which we found in the basement of the Miner building, where it had been cached with a large supply of powder. It was simply a two-inch pipe fastened to a block of wood, but it answered the purpose. Just shooting it off was pretty tame sport until somebody whose mind was still working thought of brooms. All of the nearby saloons were promptly raided for ammunition, and after that broom-handles went hurtling down the street until the powder ran out. Only the mercy of providence, with some help from the police in keeping the people off the highways, prevented numerous casualties.

By that time the party had begun to diminish in size, as the weaker brethren fell by the wayside and were laid away in their rooms, as I had promised them they would be. John Maguire, the patriarch of the party, was the last to succumb, sometime during the forenoon. No man could have asked more of wine than it did for him, nor put up a harder fight against its inevitable effect. Before oblivion began to make inroads on the celebration it had been solemnly agreed, and with oaths, that we would all meet at 6 o'clock on the evening of the Fourth to canvass the situation and ascertain whether any reasonably respectable saloon had been overlooked in our wet wanderings of the night before. But I was the only one who was at the rendezvous at the appointed time, nor did any of the others show up that night.

That seemed to put it up to me to continue the observance of the natal day which had been so happily launched, only to come a cropper when it was half finished, and there is no disguising the fact that I was feeling very uppity and all in the mode for a general disturbance of the peace. So I acquired a large American flag and sallied forth, full of patriotism and song. The fact that I couldn't sing a note made no difference. The song germ had been planted in my mind by the basses and baritones of the night before—we had no tenors with us—and I felt obliged to lift up my voice in patriotic airs. The police gave me perfect interference; anyone who sneered at my singing was arrested for disturbing the peace.

One of the places I felt called on to visit was Sam Tonkin's big concert hall, adjoining the city hall in which the central fire station was located. Sam was born in Cornwall, and his place was packed with Cousin Jacks. Quite unjustly I questioned their loyalty and invited them to prove the charge by spitting on the American flag which was waved in front of them. Failing to get a rise out of the Cornishmen, who were full of beer and good nature, I concluded to give them a lesson in patriotism by singing the national anthem. The fact that the stage was all cluttered up with chorus girls, who were cavorting gaily around in attire that was scanty even for a mining camp, made no difference.

Sam let me have my own way, of course—his decision being influenced, no doubt, to some extent by the fact that a number of friendly policemen and all of the firemen, who were Irish to a man, had forced their way into the hall, to give me their moral support. "So I chased the "bevy of beauties," as they were described on the program, into the wings, took the center of the stage and announced that I hoped the singing of the national air would have a good effect. Jake Scheller, the leader of the orchestra, gave his musicians the high sign and they tore into the song with all of the fervor of a brass band at a country fair.

If I had been yelling murder I couldn't have been heard above the blaring orchestra, but before I was half way through the congregation joined in, and the resultant racket rattled windows all over the camp. Then, with my flag over my shoulder, I proceeded on my way, in the knowledge of a duty well-performed. Several events of a somewhat similar nature were staged in more or less public places before the night was over, but the veil may be drawn over them with propriety.

As a result of that excursion into strange fields I found, when I got back to earth, that I was viewed with increased favor throughout the camp. Bill Owsley and Tom Porter and Perry Beale and others of the old bullwhackers took me to their broad bosoms and all agreed that I had done myself and the camp proud, for no amateur had ever before sung a song, however badly, from any stage in town. Wherever I was sent I met new friends and was welcomed to full brotherhood. The celebration and the patriotic outburst took rank with the year of the big wind in Ireland.

Whether Marcus Daly heard about this escapade of mine I don't know, though I assume he did, because it was on everybody's tongue for two or three days.

As usual, Mr. Daly had elected the city ticket, headed by E.O. Dugan, as mayor.

I had a run-in a little later with Jim McNichols, the city marshal, and about the whole city administration, which showed me what a fine scout the Old Man was in standing by a young reporter who was just feeling his oats. McNichols had been a hoisting engineer at the Anaconda mine and he assumed, by some involved mental process, that the fact that Mr. Daly also owned the Standard gave him the right to dictate the policy of the paper in handling police news.

I was compelled to get that idea out of his head rather forcibly. About the same time I had a little chat with Pete McArthur, the street commissioner, in which I gave him my views as to the men he should employ in his department, thinking only of Anaconda for the Capital. So Pete didn't think much of me, either. He and Jim got together and compared notes, and then called in Dugan and P.J. Harrington, chairman of the Democratic county committee, to make it stronger. They agreed to call on Mr. Daly the next evening he was in town and demand my scalp.

They figured that all they would have to do was to make the request and I would be fired. But Mr. Daly asked some questions which they found it hard to answer. When he had got to the bottom of it, the Old Man said to them, very frostily: "That was darned good advice, Pete, and if I had been in your place I would have followed it, instead of turning up my nose at it and trying to get Smith discharged. Smith is doing his work all right and is going to stay there. That's just what I've got that paper for, to keep tabs on you fellows. Now you go back and run the city hall, and try to make a better job of it than you have so far. And don't worry about Smith."

The Old Man told us of the visit of the quartette on one of his afternoon calls soon afterward, and, as he imposed no condition of secrecy, I promptly and openly declared war on McNichols in particular and the city administration in general, after serving notice to that effect, in the city hall. And that defiance came close to getting me in trouble.

AS KILLERS PURSUE ME, RIVAL UNDERTAKERS BID FOR MY BUSINESS

A few weeks later, while I was making the rounds of the gambling houses one night, an interesting new arrival in the camp was pointed out to me by Billy Weir, a grizzled faro dealer who was off duty. His name was Billy Fay and he was described as "plain poison." His face and hands had been badly burned years before in rescuing a woman from a burning hotel in Tucson, Arizona. His face never fully healed and he wore a white bandage diagonally across it, covering one eye and most of his nose and just clearing the corner of his mouth. That bandage and his reputation made him stand out in any crowd.

His hands were so gnarled and twisted that anyone who didn't know him would have ridiculed the suggestion that he could show any speed in handling a gun, yet he was one of the fastest men in the West with a six-shooter. His accuracy was deadly with either hand and, which was still more remarkable, he always used single-action guns. He was a professional gambler by occupation and a smart one, and a professional killer from choice, apparently. Gossip said he had killed up to 20 men, but always in fair fights. But there was nothing of the braggart about him nor anything in his manner to indicate that he was proud of his record. About 40 years old, he was a square-shooter and would never take an unfair advantage. He talked a little and drank less but was open to any kind of a game at any time.

I saw Fay frequently after that in the Combination, which was his chief hangout, but he seemed an excellent man to stay away from unless one was looking for trouble. A few weeks after his arrival, a bad man of an entirely different type blew into town in the person of Frank Dougherty. He was a crooked gambler of the tinhorn type and a morphine fiend; a man-killer when he was full of dope and a sneaking coward without it. Even when he was full of dope, his percentage of courage was so low that he was always looking for the best of it and he specialized in picking out easy marks for his targets. There was no authentic record of the number of men he had killed, but it was generally understood that he had quite a number of nasty murders to his discredit.

It then developed that there was a feud of long standing between Fay and Dougherty. Fay sent for Dougherty as soon as he heard of his arrival. "This camp isn't big enough for both of us, but I like it," he said. "I'll shoot it out with you right now, or any time you say, or I'll divide the camp with you."

Craving no part of the proffered gunfight, Dougherty accepted the proposition to divide the town. So it was arranged that Fay, who had first choice by right of might, should have all of the territory west of the center of Main Street while Dougherty was to confine himself to the east side. This gave Fay all of the big gambling houses while Dougherty was restricted to the cheaper resorts, which were more in his line.

"And keep on your side of Main Street," cautioned Fay. "If you get over on my side I'll sure drill you without any further notice."

I heard of this wholesale transaction in real estate soon after it was completed and, as it gave me another chance for a rap at McNichols, I jumped at it, though really I had no objection to bad men dividing the camp up into as many sections as they pleased, provided they didn't catch me in the line of fire when they opened war. So I wrote a piece, bristling with indignation, in which the city marshal was called on to chase both Fay and Dougherty out of town, as a warning to other bad men. It was argued that Butte was no longer a tough mining camp but was becoming a civilized community and that such high-handed proceedings should not be tolerated. Nothing was done about it, of course, nor was any action produced by two or three following articles of similar nature. Then, having caused McNichols enough annoyance on one subject, the matter was dropped.

The truce lasted three or four weeks, which was much longer than had been anticipated. Then Dougherty got fairly well soaked with dope one evening and crossed over to Fay's side of Main Street. He didn't stay long, for he was not entirely crazy, but his fleeting visit constituted a challenge which Fay accepted as soon as he heard of the news, which was within 10 minutes after Dougherty had departed. He first went to Wehl's gun store, in west Park Street, and bought two new Colt .45 single-action revolvers and then went gunning for Dougherty. He made the rounds of all of the cheaper resorts. But Dougherty naturally had taken to cover as soon as he heard Fay was hunting for him, and he stuck close to his hiding place.

Word of the search soon got around, and another killing was predicted. Later in the evening I was standing in the entrance of the Comique Theater talking with George Kessler, the bouncer—whom I later helped to get on the Fire Department and was blown to pieces in the dynamite explosion—when Fay came in. He passed me in the rear but Kessler whispered: "There goes Billy Fay. He's gunning for Dougherty." I turned around and saw Fay walking rapidly down the main aisle, with both hands in his overcoat pockets and looking anxiously to the right and left.

The ground floor of the Comique was open, and was packed with men and girls who sat at the tables, drinking. They were talking and carousing and the large hall, like the two floors above, was a perfect babel. But as Fay passed the talk became whispers, and a hush settled over the crowd. A seriocomic was twittering a tearful ditty on the stage to the accompaniment of the blasé orchestra, led by Harry Ganke, with the inevitable cigar between his teeth. Fay strode down the aisle, keeping his hands in his pockets, to the rail directly back of the leader.

"Stop the music," he said, quietly but in a voice with a razor edge. The peremptory tone was sufficient to impress Ganke. He kept on fiddling but turned around far enough to see the white bandage—and the music ceased, right in the middle of a bar.

"Thank you," said Billy, politely, as he swung around and faced the audience. By that time a great stillness had settled over the house. Fay's reputation was well known and there were many in the crowd who had heard he was on Dougherty's trail. Plainly enough he was in an ugly mood.

"I'm looking for that morphine-eating sonnykabick Frank Dougherty," said Fay, in a cold, hard voice, after he had looked the house over for what seemed like 10 minutes, "and I'm going to kill him on sight."

He waited a minute or two for that to sink in, while the spectators watched him, intent and motionless. Then, after raising his hands far enough for a quick draw, which brought the butts of his pistols in plain sight, he added: "I don't see Dougherty here, but...I see some of his friends, and I think I'll start on them." With that he whipped out both guns and threw them down on the crowd.

That was the one and only time I saw anything resembling a panic over a gunplay in Butte, for it was accustomed to them, but in less than a second the place was in an uproar. Fully half of the men on the ground floor made a rush for the open air, and many more who came tumbling down the stairs from the upper floors added to the confusion. In their wild scramble the mob overturned a stove, tore off one of the swinging doors and fell all over themselves when they hit the icy sidewalk. One would have thought they were all friends of Dougherty, though probably very few of them even knew him by sight. The mad rush was a great tribute to a dangerous man.

The Standard carried a story the next morning that went into all of the gory details. I was still thinking of McNichols, so the whole disgraceful proceeding was attributed to the titular head of the police department, and it was stated that it was obligatory on him to chase Fay and Dougherty out of the camp.

GUNS TURN ON THE REPORTER

That served the purpose of turning the harpoon in Jim McNichols around again, but it served another purpose that was not quite so pleasant. When I reached the office early in the afternoon, a gambler acquaintance was waiting for me. Calling me aside, he said Fay had sent him to tell that he proposed to shoot me on sight.

It was the first formal notification of that kind I had ever received, and it soon set me to thinking hard and fast. However, with an airiness that I did not feel, I cheerfully replied: "That's very kind of Billy." The gambler stared at me, as though he was trying to read what was going on in my mind, and walked away with no further comment than to "look out for myself." And it was just as well that he left promptly, for a weakness was developing in my knees about which it was not necessary for him to know.

Before I had time to collect my thoughts, a tinhorn sport, whom I knew only by sight, came in with a similar message from Dougherty. "Frank asked me to tell you that he will kill you on sight," he said, loudly so the whole office would know.

The messenger in this case was a creature of the Dougherty type. His manner was as distasteful as the word he brought. "You go back and tell Dougherty that he is just what Fay called him and that he won't shoot anybody unless he is full of hop," I told him. "Tell him too that I am not afraid of any damned dope fiend."

The first thing I did was to take my gun from my pocket and place it in my desk, with the positive intention of leaving it there until further orders. It was a beautiful Colt .45 which the police had taken away from a desperado who had cut six notches in the butt. I packed it, as a rule, only when I walked out to my rooming house, on the outskirts of the camp, early in the morning. But I had no intention of engaging in pistol practice with Mr. William Fay.

Then I sat down to think things over. I was in love with Butte and its people and did not like the idea of hitting the back trail. Furthermore, I was decidedly averse to taking it on the run from anyone. With regard to the two threats, I knew if I got it from Dougherty it would be from behind, but I figured that he would stick close to his hiding place with Fay hunting for him all of the time, so I really would not be in great danger from him. That as it turned out, was a mistake, and one which, with a little more morphine, might have had bad results.

Fay was of different caliber. I believed if I ran into him, which was the last thing I wished to do, he would disregard the notice he had sent me and ask me if I was heeled. When I told him I was not, which would assuredly be the truth, his reply would be: "Go heel yourself." Then I concluded it would be time enough to take to the tall timber. So I decided to stick it out and take a chance.

For five days I followed the usual activities of a police reporter, with pretty much all of the camp looking on and awaiting further developments, for the two friends of Fay and Dougherty had lost no time in telling of the messages they had delivered. Ed Sherman and Tom Richards, the rival undertakers, cheerfully solicited my business and Tom Porter, the coroner, assured me that if things went that far he would get the old Vigilantes together and lynch my murderer. Which was reassuring, in a way, if not exactly comforting. The police took me under their wing and rode herd on me in grand style. They were so attentive that they got in my way a bit at times, but as their purpose was altogether friendly I couldn't shoo them away. I walked the streets as usual but cut out my nightly visits to the big gambling houses, where I was certain to encounter Fay, and engaged in no day dreams while I was walking around.

On the third night, early in the morning I started from the corner of Main and Park Streets, which was the liveliest intersection in the camp, to walk one block east to Arizona Street. One of the cops at the corner suggested that he accompany me, but I laughed at him; the south side of Park Street was devoted entirely to saloons, and was much busier than in the daytime, and there were several more on the north side.

Hell With the Lid Off

At the opening of City Hall part way down the block were telegraph and telephone poles set closely together so that they formed a recess on the east side. Through a narrow irregular crack between the two poles, I thought I saw something move as I approached them. Instantly I thought Dougherty was lying in wait for me, as that would be just his kind of a game. It was then too late to turn around without giving him a wide back for a target at close range and a fine chance for a getaway up the dark alley. So I kept on walking, ready to jump at the slightest suspicious sound. I did not turn my head as I passed the suspected hiding place—though my right ear was stretched out to all of two feet—nor did I look around after I passed it.

Nothing happened.

On the sixth day I visited police headquarters, as usual, before starting out on my rounds. The city marshal had a very red face and was so excited about something that he was full of talk. Billy (W.J.) Naughten, the police judge, was sitting on a table, swinging his feet and looking quite self-conscious. From them I learned that Fay and Dougherty had both sent them word that they would kill them on sight, having been tipped off that McNichols had at last awakened and was planning to round them up and chase them out of town. And McNichols, brave man that he was, had telephoned out to his cops to bring both of them in, and intended to remain right where he was, safely in his office, until the outlaws were both in jail.

I laughed at them. "They sent me that word six days ago," I told them, "but I couldn't get you stirred up about it. You're a grand and noble head of the police department."

Both men were picked up late in the afternoon and taken to the city jail. Dougherty was locked up in the men's department while Fay was confined in the women's section. There were grated doors to each department which faced each other across an outer office. I went out to look them over. Fay was not in sight but Dougherty was standing at the door, wearing a sickly smile. He told me the police were chasing them out of the camp and asked me to shake hands with him, but I refused. He wanted to know why, and I told him it was because he was just what Fay had called him.

"You ought not to talk to me like that," he said. "I saved your life the other night."

"Yes? You were hiding behind those poles in front of Gallick's liquor store, weren't you?" I asked him. When his eyes widened in surprise I inquired as to how he was going to work it.

"I had it all planned," he replied. "When you were close enough I was going to step out and spit in your face. Then, when you grabbed for me I was going to shoot you, and make it a case of self-defense."

"Why didn't you try it?"

"Oh, I thought you were too good a fellow to kill thataway."

"Shucks! You didn't shoot because you didn't have enough dope in you, which was the way I figured it. You're just a coward and a skunk."

Turning my back on Dougherty I saw Fay standing at the barred door on the other side of the lobby. He was smiling broadly and apparently had heard all that had been said. Beckoning me to him, with a nod of the head, he asked me if I would shake hands with him.

"Sure," and I extended my hand, which he took in his twisted fingers with a surprisingly strong grip.

He wanted to know why I was so willing to shake hands with him when I wouldn't with Dougherty, and I told him just how I had them sized up, and what he would be likely to do if I met him.

Fay smiled and nodded approval. "Yes, I would have done that," he said. After a moment of thoughtfulness he added: "They are going to let us out of here pretty soon. If you will come to my room with me, I'll give you a good story."

I told him I would be waiting for him. As I was leaving the jail with him, two hours after Dougherty had been released, Jim Leyden, the chief of police, called me back to ask where

I was going. When I told him he said: "Man, you're crazy. He'll shoot you full of holes."

I told him that Fay wouldn't do any shooting, but Jim lacked some of my optimism. When he was unable to shake my determination to get what I wanted, he stationed half a dozen cops around the rooming house in which Fay was making his farewell appearance in Butte, though I knew nothing about this arrangement until after it was all over.

In his room Fay talked fully and frankly. He seemed anxious to present his side of the case and all questions were answered freely. He told about his feud with Dougherty, which had its origin in a woman acquaintance of Fay's who had been handed a dirty deal by Frank the Dope.

"When Dougherty gets his," he said, "it will be from behind, just as he has given it to all of the men he has killed."

I asked Fay how many men he had shot.

"Some say 10 and others about 20. I think the latter figure is an exaggeration, but it may be right. But I never shot a man except in a fair fight, and nearly all the fights I have had were started in the hope that I would be the one to die," he replied.

"People say I'm a brave man but I know I'm not. As a matter of cold fact, I'm a coward; as big a coward as Dougherty, really, though not the same kind. My life is a continual torture to me," he said, pulling the bandage far enough back from his face to show me that it had never healed.

"Every day I wish many times that I were dead. I have looked down the barrel of a six-shooter a thousand times, with the gun cocked and my thumb on the trigger. But I've never had the nerve enough to fire. That proves that I'm a coward, doesn't it? It does to me anyway."

"Because I haven't the courage to kill myself I've tried to get myself killed by other men. With my face hurting like the devil and a few drinks in me, I've deliberately picked quarrels with men I knew were quick on the trigger with the idea of committing suicide that way. Then self-preservation, which is the strongest natural law, would assert itself and

I would go for my own gun. And the hell of it has been that I always got in the first shot. I trained myself to be fast with a gun after I was hurt, and I never have been badly hurt by a bullet. Someday, though, I will meet a man who is faster than I am, and then I will get mine. And I will really be glad when that time comes. If I had half the nerve people think I have I would have killed myself long ago. But before I go I would like to get Dougherty."

As I was leaving Fay's room he called out, as an afterthought; "Tell Durston I said it was all right to use that story."

I asked him what he meant, at the same time assuring him that we did not need his consent to print stuff in the Standard.

"That is true enough in the Butte office," he said, "but I've got Durston scared stiff and he won't print that story unless you tell him I said he could."

He offered no further explanation and I asked for none, as I was in a hurry to get back to the office with the makings of a bully yarn. I thought he was kidding himself, and told him so. What had happened, though I did not know of it until later, was that Fay had been in Anaconda a couple of weeks before, just after one of my stories aimed at McNichols was printed, and took occasion to call on the eminent editor. Fay walked in and introduced himself.

"I am Billy Fay," he said, "and you're Durston, the editor of this paper. The Standard has had a hell of a lot to say about me recently, and I just came in to tell you that if my name ever appears in your paper again, in any connection, I will kill you. There is a big fellow in Butte named Smith that I will get, too, but I am going to kill you, for you are responsible for everything you print."

Durston promptly assured him that his name would never again appear in the Standard. But, naturally enough, he failed to tell everyone about his visitor, contenting himself with looking over the Butte proofs every night.

In blissful ignorance of this occurrence, I wrote a column and a half story about the exit of Fay and Dougherty and the

Hell With the Lid Off

talk with Fay and put it on the wire. Wally agreed that it was quite unnecessary to transmit Fay's message to Durston, so there was no reference to it.

Durston, however, was sitting in his room in the Montana Hotel, across the street from the Standard office, waiting for the first paper off the press. When it was delivered to him the first thing he saw, leading the first page, was a long story about his friend Bill Fay. Throwing an overcoat over his pajamas, but without waiting to exchange his slippers for shoes, he dashed across the street through two feet of snow, with the thermometer 10 below zero, and ordered the presses stopped and the Fay story killed. When I reached the office the next afternoon, Durston had Wally on the telephone and was excitedly demanding that I be fired instantly for "trying to get him killed." Wally told him just what had happened and backed me up properly but Durston was so fussed up about it, and so insistent that I be discharged that he was finally compelled to take the matter up with Mr. Daly to save my job. Mr. Daly chuckled and allowed it was a good joke on Durston. And on the following morning the Fay story was published.

Ten days later, Dougherty was killed over in Helena while running away from a crap game in which he had been accused of skullduggery. He was shot through the back of the head, just as Fay had predicted. Fay left the camp within an hour after our talk and was never heard from again, as far as any of his friends in the camp ever knew. Wherever he went, I hope Fate was kinder to him than he was to himself.

Editor's note. Billy Fay died, in Ogden, Utah, in the summer of 1898. News stories at the time echo Smith's characterization, albeit sympathetic, of a dangerous man. An account in the Helena Independent noted Fay's "scrupulous concealment of part of his face" and his skills in fanning his "enormous" pistol with his opposite hand. "He had a violent streak, known for kicking over gaming tables and routinely being run out of town."

The story concludes. "At last he died as ordinary men, of fever. The predictions of those who knew him that he would come to a violent end were unfulfilled."

CHAPTER 3
GOD V. THE DEVIL BRINGS OUT THE TOWN

In the shabby little church, gamblers and prostitutes crowded up against men of religion and dainty little women

In saloons and gambling houses, they spoke of the 'he-man parson who wasn't afraid'

A plagiarizing preacher gets his due

Butte probably is the only city in the country which has a large and handsome church for which an atheist, and his violent abuse of God and the Bible, was responsible. Construction followed close on a sensational incident that caused more animated conversation, in places where there was an unwritten law against the mention of church or religion, that would have resulted from half a dozen man-killings. The incident propelled a two-fisted young parson, who had been faithfully riding herd on a straggling and struggling little congregation, on his way to much more than local fame, with a devoted force of fighting enthusiasts at his back.

The Butte office of the Standard was in a long room, originally intended for a store, on the ground floor on west Broadway, opposite the city hall and close to the center of the camp's gambling and commercial activities. The business office was in front and the city room in the rear, with only a railing for a dividing line. The editorial end never closed before 3 o'clock in the morning, and late at night it was a popular gathering place for congenial souls: an old prospector, in some ways the most interesting type in the country and a never-ending source of gossip, just back from a trip into the hills with only a packhorse for a companion; mining men; prize fighters, wrestling and rock drilling experts; faro dealers off duty; gamblers with tales of big winnings or losses; doctors who came in to report births or deaths and remained to talk—they all were among those who yielded to the magnetism of a newspaper office at night. The latchstring was always out to interesting people.

Pests occasionally took advantage of this open-door policy. One of the worst of these was William Leff, who came into the world wailing and kept right at it. Nothing was right with the world and nothing suited him. There was no sun by day or stars at night, no changing seasons, no seed-time and harvest. Everything in the universe required readjustment and it was his notion that it was up to him to do the fixing. He had a good education but was short on all of the other qualifications for his self-assumed job.

His hair was red, his disposition the same and he packed a vicious tongue and a raucous voice. He came in the first time to protest about the report of a sermon. Somebody on the paper saw a story in him and printed some of the things he said, more with the idea of poking fun at him than for their news value. With no suspicion that he had been ridiculed, he assumed that his views were of some importance. So, waiving the formality of an invitation, he returned at intervals to turn them loose. He was cocksure of many things but that of which he was most certain was that there was no God and that anyone who believed in the existence of a supreme being was an ass, to put it politely. Hating everything that was good, his bitterest dislike was reserved for God and the Bible. On those subjects he was violently verbose.

I had seen and heard him around the office on several occasions, but I spent most of the time on the outside, where things were happening. I interposed no objection to his ravings for the additional reason that I was getting no salary for supervising the spiritual atmosphere of the news shop. He didn't seem worth bothering about. However, as he could find no other audience, he felt called on to visit our office one night, just as I was writing a big story.

Airily disregarding a warning scowl I handed him in lieu of an invitation, he sat down at the end of my desk and proceeded to deliver a lecture to all and sundry on the silliness of the God theory and the nastiness of the Bible. For some reason—perhaps because I had openly ignored him in his previous harangues and because all zealots derive their greatest joy from the conversion of scoffers—he made me the chief target for his sacrileges. His rasping voice soon had my nerves at the breaking point.

"The Bible is a filthy book," he shouted. "I will give $100 in gold to any minister who will read a chapter from it that I select to his congregation from his pulpit."

That gave me a fine opening. I told him he was a red-headed liar and worse. When the epithet I used failed to start a fight I continued: "Maybe you think, from the language I sometimes use that I don't believe in the Bible, but I do. But it has to be intelligently read, which is why you can't understand it. You've made your bluff; now fill your hand or lay it down. Either put up your $100 or get to hell out of here and stay out."

Leff glared at me for a moment. Then without a word, he stamped out of the office. We all thought we were through with him, but that idea was waterlogged. Just as I finished the story he had interfered with he returned, with five $20 gold pieces in a leather bag.

"There's my money," he shouted triumphantly. "That makes my end of it good. Now you find some minister who will make good on your end of it, if you can."

Drawing up articles of agreement for prize fights, wrestling matches and rock-drilling contests was part of my job, so I made this a sporting proposition in fact and put it in writing, to avoid any misunderstanding. It was a plain and simple document, free from any complicating clauses. Leff signed three copies of the agreement and his signature was properly witnessed. Our business office was closed for the night so I placed the money for safekeeping overnight in the safe in Ernest Lange's saloon next door. That seemed an odd place to deposit church funds, for I considered the bet as good as won, but saloons and gambling houses were the only places with strong boxes that were open so late at night.

The proprietor displayed surprising interest when I explained the nature of the bet for which I was holding the stakes. After a moment of serious thought, which probably covered both retrospection and introspection, he called everybody up to the bar. He told, briefly, of the wager that had just been concluded and announced that the drinks were on the house.

"We'll drink," he said, "to the health of the sky-pilot who has enough guts to soak that damned atheist." That little incident brought out the spirit of the camp and was a good indication of what was to follow.

OH YE MEN OF LITTLE FAITH

Congratulating myself on having secured a big, exclusive story so easily, I sallied forth the next day, full of enthusiasm, to round it out. I supposed that any minister would be glad to accept the proposition of the blasphemous Leff, for here was a direct and public challenge to the faith that was in him and the religion he preached. Furthermore, the defending clergyman was bound to get a lot of free publicity, to which none of the cloth was at all averse. And I knew of no church in the camp that would not be delighted to have $100 added to its slim treasury with so little effort to secure it. These arguments seemed convincing enough but, as was soon demonstrated, they merely proved that I knew very little about the ministers of Butte.

Convenience counted for more than creed, and the first man I called on was Rev. S.C. Blackiston, rector of the Protestant Episcopal church, whose residence I passed daily on my way to the office. Mr. Blackiston was a nice, kindly old gentleman, who knew the Bible backwards and could recite all of the prayers and rituals and thingamajigs of his church in his sleep. He was a profound student and the possessor of much knowledge. The only thing he didn't know much about, as it developed, was human nature.

As Leff's defiant proposal was put before him, a look of something much like terror came over his face and he held up his hands in horror. What, engage in a public argument about God and the Bible with an atheist? Never! It was nothing short of an outrage to even suggest such a thing. Not that he blamed me at all, of course, for that was a part of my newspaper work, but it was an outrage just the same. No! A whole fistful of nos. All of the nos there were in the world, in fact.

Disappointed because of the additional legwork involved on a July day, but not discouraged, I next visited the pastor of the Christian church, who lived only a few blocks away. He had one of the largest congregations in the camp and only a few weeks before had dedicated a fine new church of which he was very proud. I had written several columns about the ceremonies connected with the opening of his new building and we had become quite friendly. He liked to see his name in print as much as any theatrical producer or actor. So I took it for granted that he would jump at the chance to secure some additional publicity, and at the same time prove his faith by his works. To my astonishment he took the same view that had been so warmly expressed by his Episcopal brother. He was good-natured about it, but as firm as the rock of St. Peter.

My opinion of the clergymen of Butte was going down, and it sank still lower when I found that Rev. John E. Squires, the Methodist Episcopal Church South minister, and Rev. Frank E. Brush, of the Mountain View M.E. Church, were of the same mind. Mr. Brush was comparatively a newcomer in the camp and full of brash ways and a high-hat disposition. He was not satisfied with rejecting my proposal with all of the scorn he had handy but proceeded to lecture me on my own wickedness, in promoting such a disgraceful proceeding, in return for which I told him to go to the devil. As a further compensation for his presumptuousness and lack of faith I had the very great pleasure of bringing about his downfall and discomfiture not long afterward.

There were not a whole lot of churches in Butte in those days and the supply of potential ammunition for my side of the battle was running dangerously low. I knew Father Van de Van, of St. Patrick's Church, would never entertain the proposal. Nor would Dr. Maurice Eisenberg, the Jewish Rabbi, who had no regular church, and who soon would leave his little flock to do the best it could and move to New York to make a fortune on Wall Street. The only other minister who was available was Rev. E.J. Groeneveld, of the First Presbyterian church, a shabby little frame building at the corner of Broadway and Idaho Streets. I had passed his church many times but had never been inside of it.

I had met Rev. Groeneveld several times and rather liked him. He was a quiet, unobtrusive chap, who knew his own mind and was not afraid to speak it. The only reason I had left him to the last was because he lived away up on top of the hill, and it was a hot day. But, with all of the other clergymen hoisting the white flag, in very cowardly and disgraceful fashion as it seemed to me, there was nothing to do but trudge skyward. By the time I reached the manse I was plenty hot, inside and out. I found him in his study, at the side of the house. He saw me through the screen door and beckoned me in.

"Say," I said, with a manner that must have appeared

rude, "are you ashamed of the book out of which you are making your living?"

"What do you mean?" he replied, smiling and not at all disturbed. "The Bible?"

"Yes, the Bible."

"No, of course not. Why?"

"Well, a red-headed so and so of an atheist offers $100 to any minister who will read from the pulpit a chapter that he selects. He claims the Bible is a filthy book and that is his way of proving it. And every other damned sky-pilot in the camp practically admits he is right by refusing to call his bluff. How about you?"

"I'll call it," said Groeneveld, still smiling, without raising his voice and without a second's hesitation. "There is nothing in the Bible that I am afraid to read, anywhere at any time." He was not at all agitated and his whole manner indicated that, to his mind, it was a very simple proposition and required no serious consideration. The Bible had been attacked. He was there to defend it. That was the natural thing for him to do and he assumed no heroic pose.

"You mean you'll go through with it, then?"

"Certainly. I know of several places where we can use $100 to good advantage."

"You can paint your church, for one thing," I observed.

"Yes. But it will buy a lot of books for our Sunday school, and we need them."

Groeneveld, still smiling, affixed his signature, which I witnessed, to the three copies of the articles of agreement, and retained one of them. I marched exultantly down the hill to herald the news to the world that was Butte.

With a view to arousing a proper degree of popular interest, and at the same time emphasizing the fighting nature of the young parson who lived on the hill—in which, as one who had been raised in the Presbyterian faith, I felt something of personal pride—I divided the story into three parts, even though we were far from Gaul. The first one told of the challenge issued by Leff, with enough about his atheistic views to make a good yarn. The second day's section recited the refusals of the Episcopal, Christian, Methodist and Baptist ministers to take up the gauntlet with the reasons they had given for declining to defend their faith. Considerable space was given to the follower of John Wesley—though trailing the founder of Methodism far in the rear—and his bombastic discourse on newspaper ethics and the moral code, which later soon came back to haunt him.

Publication of these facts put all four of the fearsome fathers in rather a bad way. They were called on for explanations which they could not make clear, and their smug satisfaction with themselves was quickly dissipated under a rain of sarcastic comment from contributing members of their congregations. They realized then that they had made a mistake, but it was too late for them to correct it.

The two introductory stories created a great deal of talk and provided a perfect background for the third one, which proclaimed the fact that in the Rev. E.J. Groeneveld, the camp had one minister who had the courage of his convictions and was prepared to champion the Bible at all times and against all comers, with no holds barred. His unhesitating acceptance of the atheist's challenge and the manner of it were fully set forth, in contrast with the demurs and remonstrance of the other clergymen.

Groeneveld was comparatively unknown up to that time, for his congregation was small and the term of his residence had been short. But before the end of the day on which the third story was printed, he was being more talked about than any other man in the camp, and in circles where no minister of the gospel had ever before been seriously considered or discussed. He made a dynamic appeal to the popular imagination in a perfectly natural way. The people always have admired a fighter, and always will. Here was a fighting parson, the highest and finest type of battler. Though still a tenderfoot, as gauged by the date of his arrival in the camp, his spirit was the spirit of Butte. And, though few knew him, even by sight, the camp developed a great liking for him.

In compliance with the terms for his challenge, Leff specified the 15th chapter of Leviticus, on which chloride of lime could well be used, as the one that was to be read. "I thought that would be it," said Groeneveld when he was advised of the selection. But he was quite unruffled about it. And as the youngsters in his Sunday school, who were his greatest friends, were in urgent need of the books the atheist's money would furnish them, he announced that he would read the bugaboo chapter at the regular service on the following Sunday evening, June 5th 1892. That was but only two days away. This information was passed on to a public that was displaying increasing interest, and the stage was all set for what was designated as "the battle between God and the devil."

Anticipating an unusually large attendance at the unique service, I walked out to the fearless parson's little congregational corral early on Sunday evening to be sure of a good seat, to which the stakeholder in any contest is always entitled. But as soon as I came within sight of the church all thoughts of a ring-side seat vanished. I was aware of all the talk my stories had generated. And I knew the extent to which the sporting blood of the camp had been stirred by the blatant challenge of the blasphemous atheist and the manner of its acceptance. But I was altogether unprepared for the situation I found.

GOD'S TRIUMPH

The shabby little church had become a shrine!

Every seat was occupied, probably for the first time in its history, and the open space near the door was tightly packed with standees of both sexes. Gamblers and prostitutes, attracted by the spirit of context or drawn by the memories of other days, were crowded against religious men and dainty women. There was no drawing away from soiled contacts. That would have been impossible anyway, but there seemed to be no such pharisaical disposition. Perhaps a thousand people, who had arrived early but too late to gain a foothold on the inside, were molded together outside of the church, peering intently through the open windows.

The outside crowd included faro dealers and sporting men of all grades, who had come to pay their tribute to a fighter. Their hats were off, as an outward sign of their respect, and the fact that they were often quite profane in their quiet comments among themselves while waiting for the service to begin—in remarks about the "damned good sport of a parson" and what a blankety blank blank the atheist was—made no difference. Over the whole scene was an air of great reverence; the influence of the quiet, stout-hearted minister proved its power.

At the first attempt I made to get close to the church I met with no success. When I tried to force my way through the crowd at one of the windows, I was told by a dozen subdued voices, to "get to hell out of here." It was only after I had explained that I was holding the stakes for the contest and that the fight probably would not go on unless the parson saw the bag of gold I was carrying that I was extended the privilege of a seat in a window, close to the pulpit. Even then I needed the help of two or three policemen to get to it.

The first thing I saw was the redhead who'd caused all the excitement. Leff had a seat in the first row of pews, directly in front of the pulpit. He must have arrived at the church about 4 o'clock in the afternoon. I caught Groeneveld's eye and held up the little bag of gold. He smiled broadly and waved his hand. Red Head turned his head and frowned fiercely.

When the minister started to read the chapter that had been selected for him, he took the articles of agreement from his coat pocket and laid them down beside the Bible, unostentatiously but with an evident purpose of preventing any misunderstanding. So far as I have been able to learn, and I have made many inquiries through the church sources, that was the only occasion on which a lesson has been read from a pulpit under such conditions.

After he had read a few verses Groeneveld paused to explain the real meanings, as he understood them. Red Head was on his feet instantly, protesting.

"Sit down," commanded the preacher, in a voice that was surprisingly stern. "You are in the house of God and you must behave yourself. I am reading this chapter, word for word, just as it is printed here and that is all I am required to do. I have the articles of agreement right here and they are very plain. They do not restrict me in any explanations I care to make."

Leff subsided, grumblingly. A little farther along, the parson again stopped his reading to elucidate a point that he did not think was clear, and again the atheist jumped up to enter an objection.

"If you don't sit down and keep quiet," said Groeneveld, pointing a steady finger at him, "I'll have you thrown out." He said it as though he meant it, and Leff gave up the fight.

As soon as the reading of the chapter was concluded, Red Head made an unceremonious bolt for the door. The crowd provided a passageway for him. When he reached the door, the outside throng welcomed him with derisive hoots and curses, and he was expedited in his descent of half a dozen steps by several kicks from the rear. He disappeared in the night and was never seen in Butte again. Where he came from or where he went, no one ever knew.

Willing hands reached out to pass the prize along to the parson when he finished the last verse and closed the Bible. The strangely variegated congregation applauded him heartily and the crowd outside raised a cheer that was loud and long. Then, while the people on the inside remained for the rest of the service—and sang Onward Christian Soldiers with a roar that could have been heard for a mile—the multitude melted away. Faro dealers and gamblers returned to their tables and saloon-keepers went back to their bars, and the ordinary Sunday night activities of the camp were resumed. But all over town gambling games were checked and drinking bouts were interrupted while men who had not attended anything like a religious service for many years stopped to talk of that "he-man of a parson who wasn't afraid."

There was no stopping Groeneveld after that. His congregation grew swiftly. Men who had long forgotten that they possessed a spiritual nature went to hear him preach a religion they could understand and believe. He neither minced words nor mouthed them, and the camp liked that as much as it admired his courage and his quiet modesty. The old bullwhackers worshipped no idols, nor did those who first came to live among them, but the parson who was not afraid became as much of a popular hero as the camp ever had—albeit that other superb battler, albeit in altogether different arenas—Marcus Daly.

I happened to be talking with the proprietor of one of the biggest gambling houses not long after Leff had been disposed of. The big games were opening up and he was just taking the main bankroll, a large drawer filled with gold pieces, out of the safe.

"You know," he said, with a nod at the bankroll, "Groeneveld can have any part of that he wants when he wants to build a new church. I make my money a whole lot easier than he does, but he's a damned sight better man. Didn't he rip that sonnykabick atheist up one side and down the other, though?

"I used to go to church when I was a kid. I can't go now, of course, for Sunday is our biggest day, and a gambler in church would look funny. But I was there when he took the hide off that red-headed dog and I'm strong for him. He sure is gaited right."

It was not a great while after that until a new and much larger church was needed, to satisfy the demands of a steadily increasing attendance and provide room for the Sunday school, which was Groeneveld's pride. With support from all sides and all classes, the Presbyterians built the largest and finest church in town of enduring brick and granite, compared with which the little frame structure looked like a shanty. Dr. Groeneveld had many calls after that, from other and larger cities with greater compensation in cash, but he ignored them all. He knew Butte and loved its wild, wide-open days. And Butte knew and loved him. And he is still preaching in the handsome church that is a lasting monument to his courage and looking forward to celebrating his golden anniversary two years from now. But his spirit is still as young as it was when he put the quietus on the noisy Leff.

A CLERICAL PLAGIARIST EXPOSED

Soon after, one of the ministers made an effort to regain some of his lost prestige. With a blare of trumpets, the Rev. William Rollins announced a series of sermons on "Woman." News is news, no matter where it comes from, and the press has a constant yearning for stuff with a feminine appeal. So we ran extracts from, or resumes of, some of these discourses on Monday mornings, when we were short of murders, suicides or mining accidents, and we gave them a good deal of space.

The minister's words ran in addition to our "sermons" from the Rev. Jerry Rounder which, in fact, were written by Wally Walsworth, my boss in the newsroom, whenever sluff games did not interfere, on various topics of the day. And they were so cleverly done that they fooled a lot of people all of the time. The public thought they were delivered in a deserted church in the old placer diggings, and we often heard of people going down there and trying to find the Rev. Rounder. They even fooled Johnny MacMurray, of the rival Inter Mountain paper—owned by Lee Mantle, a Republican businessman who would become a U.S. senator. One Monday morning that Wally missed fire, MacMurray inquired as to where Mr. Rounder lived so that he could get his sermon.

The sermons on "Woman" served the minister's purpose by attracting some attention and were made the subject of conversation by churchgoers. They surprised me, for they displayed a fount of knowledge and a breadth of vision which I did not believe the clergyman possessed, and a beauty of expression of which I had not considered him capable.

Dr. Groeneveld and I met by chance one afternoon and stopped to talk about matters and things. The "Woman" sermons were mentioned and I expressed my opinion of their supposed author with much force and feeling. Groeneveld smiled in approval.

"He's stealing those sermons, you know," he said, with a twinkle in his eye.

Instantly I cheered up, as the mystery that had been puzzling me began to clear. "No, I didn't know it," I said. "Where is he stealing them from?"

"From a book of Bristol's sermons," he said, referring to the oft-quoted Dr. Frank Bristol, a man who preaches to presidents.

"Have you the book?"

"Yes," he replied.

"Fine and grand and noble. Let's go and get it."

Comparisons of the book of sermons with the accounts we had printed of those that had been delivered by the minister left no doubt about the burglary, as far as the theft of ideas was concerned. But it was necessary to make the case complete. Knowing that Rollins wrote his sermons out in longhand and read them, to save himself the trouble of memorizing them and speaking from notes, I did not get to his church on the following Sunday evening until about the end of the service. Explaining my late arrival I asked the minister to let me have his sermon so that I could run a good story about it in the morning. Still resentful of my remarks to and about him in connection with the case of Leff, he wanted publicity more than he wished to vent his spite. So, with reluctance, he acceded to my request.

On comparing this sermon with those in the book it was found to be an exact copy of one that had been delivered by Dr. Bristol years before. Not a word had been changed. The two were identical, even to their punctuation. The Standard the next morning printed the two sermons, side by side. At the top of one column appeared: "So many years ago, at his tabernacle in London, Dr. Frank Bristol said:" At the top of

Hell With the Lid Off

the companion column was printed: "Last night at our local church the pastor said:"

The minister was quite peeved when I visited him the next day to return the sermon he had copied so carefully from the Bristol book and ask him a few questions. But even after my story ran, as an evidence of his mentality, he did not appear to realize the enormity of his sin.

"Well, what have you to say about it?" I inquired.

"What have I to say about what?"

"About stealing Dr. Bristol's stuff."

"I wouldn't call that stealing."

"No? What would you call it then?"

"He squirmed around and evaded the question for some time but I insisted that he make some direct answer to it. Finally he said:

"I would call it royal seizure of thought."

"Seizure of words, commas and periods, too, wasn't it?"

He repeated that "royal seizure of thought" was the correct definition. And that was all he had to say.

"Royal seizure" seemed a good line, so we adopted it on the Standard for use in all cases involving theft. "John Doe was sent to jail for 10 days for the royal seizure of a pair of trousers belonging to Richard Roe," was the way it would appear in a story on police court proceedings. Wherever "theft" or "'burglary" or "larceny" would ordinarily be used we substituted "royal seizure."

In about a month, Rollins offered his resignation. It was immediately accepted, and he went out in search of new fields—but the reporter he had so vigorously lectured on ethics, remained. His departure was much like that of the Leff. It seemed a proper ending for both of them.

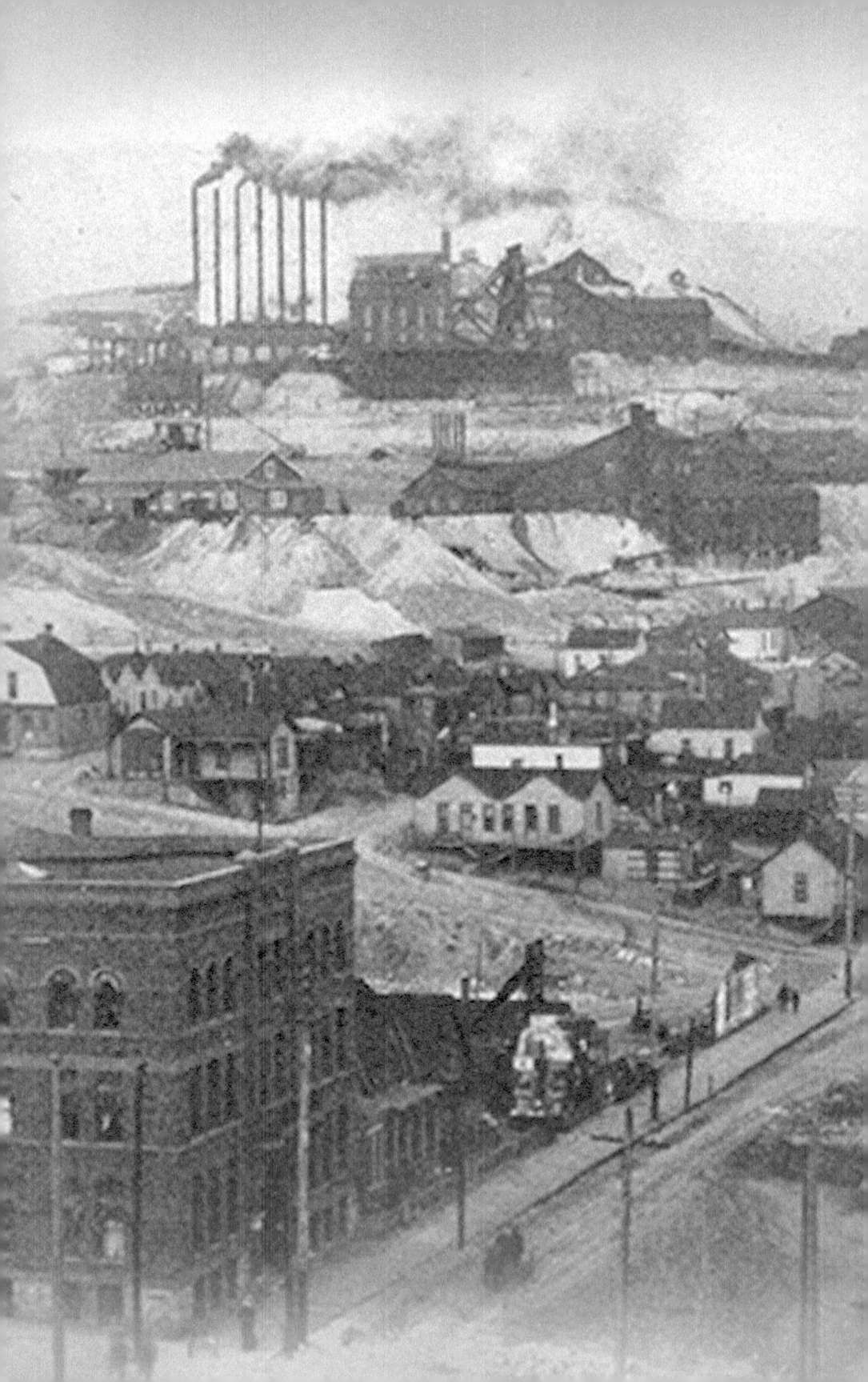

CHAPTER 4
HONEST SPORT

The women of Galena Street

Rolling grindstones down Main Street

The real treasures of Butte—its mineral wealth and its great soul, which was evidenced in the case of the fanatical atheist—were buried deep underground. One had to search for them and they were brought to light only through patient and understanding effort or, occasionally, by a streak of luck. All of the surface indications were unholy and unwholesome to the cultured visiting eye or to those accustomed only to the drab existence of the effete East.

I was looking out over the camp one night from the rooms of the Oro Plata Club in the Owsley block—the first "skyscraper," built by Bill Owsley, one of the noblest of the old bullwhackers. He equipped it with a real elevator running to all of its five floors. I was a tenderfoot who had been intently studying the animated scene, saloons and bawdy houses in the immediate foreground. A mile away from down in the flat, smelters belched thick yellow smoke when cars of boiling slag were dumped, illuminating the heavens with a red glare. I sententiously unburdened myself of the verdict that this town certainly looks like hell with the lid off.

The description was considered perfect. In the bright and palmy days of Butte, Easterners charged it with being not only the wickedest town in the United States but with the added offense of boasting of that fact. That was never literally true. What Butte was proud of, and perhaps did boast of at times for the benefit of its open-mouthed guests, was the frankness that governed every phase of its life and all of its activities. The only thing that was barred was dishonesty. And that inflexible rule was really the only thing that, barring the obvious, differentiated Butte from the Eastern cities from which came its chief critics. Everything had to be absolutely on the square. That was an inheritance from the noble old Vigilantes, who understood what it meant to "meet on the level and part on the square." It was that bond that held them together so firmly and protected all of their secrets.

Subject only to that restriction, everything was wide open, with never a thought of concealment. Strangers looked only for what they described as vice. Naturally, they saw nothing else. They needed no guide to aid them in their search nor were they forced to strain their eyes. The center of the camp was thickly spotted with whole blocks occupied entirely by saloons and gambling houses, burlesque theaters and concert halls, hurdy-gurdies for public dancing and houses of prostitution.

Galena Street, only one block from the heart of the business district, was given over exclusively to narrow little cribs consisting of three rooms, one behind the other tightly wedged together, where women sat in the windows soliciting trade. They wore much less clothing than the flapper of today and occasionally, under a free and easy administration and on a hot summer night, they wore none at all. But they were not allowed to solicit in the street and there was no law compelling any man to enter their abodes against his will. Mercury Street, one block below, was filled with larger and more pretentious houses of the same kind. Here the blinds were drawn and the doors were closed but there was no other difference, except in the prices.

The Galena Street women were of all colors and all shades. They came from all countries and climes, with a considerable sprinkling of Chinese and Japanese among them. Some of them were expert thieves and complaints of robberies were frequent. Most of the wails came from tenderfeet who, unaccustomed to the ways of the West, were the easiest victims, though the women played no favorites in their pilfering. All of the dens were connected by secret panels with the adjoining houses.

When a woman robbed a visitor, if he was of the type who was likely to "squawk," she would slip his roll to the girl in the next crib as soon as he closed the door, on his way out. If it was a large roll she would ask that it be passed on down the line. Consequently, by the time the victim discovered his loss and found a policeman and located the house in which he had been robbed—which was not a simple matter for they all looked alike—his money might be eight or ten doors away. And the women could keep passing it along faster than the police could search the houses. Therefore, in the absence of any tangible evidence of the robbery, there were few arrests as compared with the number of robberies.

These Galena Street shacks, for which an exorbitant rent was charged, were largely owned by a prominent politician, as I discovered more or less by accident. There was nothing wrong about that, of course, except that the politician was a prominent church man of the goody-goody type, who was never seen on Galena Street nor in the company of any men who went there, except reporters. There was no suspicion that a considerable part of his income came from the disgraceful cribs.

A POCKET-PICKING PROSTITUTE

The queen of all the women thieves was Jew Jess. Her fingers were so smooth and skilled and swift that she could rob a man while he had both eyes on her. She proved her claim to her title one night to the humiliation of a San Francisco detective, noted in his home town for his shrewdness, who had come to Butte after a prisoner. He had heard about the clever crooks of Galena Street and expressed a desire to look them over. City detective Jere "The Wise" Murphy, who would become chief of police, was piloting him around and was glad to comply with his wish and add to his entertainment. But Jere good-naturedly suggested that he keep his hand on his watch while they were visiting around. At that the Californian bristled. His personal and professional pride, and his pride in the city that burned but did not quake, were being slurred and scraped.

"Huh," said he, with fine scorn, "quit your kidding. We have the smartest female thieves in the world right in San Francisco. They never have touched me, and it's a cinch that you haven't any here who can come close to robbing me."

"Righto," replied Jere, with a cheerful smile in which the Californian might have seen something of a menace if he had looked carefully. Murphy hurried word to Jess that he was bringing in a man who he wanted her to rob of everything but his shoes. But it was only a joke and everything must be returned. Then Jere escorted the fly into the spider's parlor. Jess sat in the detective's lap and played with his hair. She was careful to keep her hands in plain sight, for he was watching her closely. He told her about the extremely clever women thieves they had in San Francisco, and Jess registered wonderment at their boasted smartness. Then the two detectives went away.

"What time is it?" innocently inquired Jere when they were in the street. The Californian reached for his watch. Gone. So were his wallet, his railroad ticket and the pin on his tie, as he discovered on frisking himself.

"That's funny," observed Jere, with apparent sympathy. "You could not have been robbed in Butte. Maybe you left them in your hotel."

"I don't leave things in my room. That woman has them," said the San Franciscan, his manner much subdued. "Let's go back."

Jess welcomed their return visit with a smile in which there was no trace of guile. She ordered drinks served and playfully resumed her seat on the visitor's knee.

"I want the things you stole from me," he announced. Jess gave him a blank stare and asked what he meant. He impatiently enumerated the missing articles. "You've got 'em. Give 'em back," he demanded.

Jess raised her hands to heaven in protest. She also moved them in other directions, but so swiftly that her visitor's eye could not follow them. The Californian consented to have a drink, anyway, and while his mind was partly diverted by the liquor she completed the switch.

"Come on, I'm tired of this foolishness," said the humbled sleuth, rising to his feet. "Give me my things."

"You've got them all," was the laughing response.

Incredulously the detective felt for his watch. It was where it ought to be. So were his wallet, his train ticket and even the pin in his tie.

"Well I'll be damned. I thought we had the cleverest pickpockets in the world in San Francisco, but you've got them all skinned."

"Some confession for any Californian to make," commented the very well satisfied Jere. "Let's have another drink and then we'll go."

In return for that little entertainment, Mr. Murphy had trouble with his hearing when the next man charged Jess with having rolled him. But after that she was subject to arrest whenever the police considered they had a good case against her.

Houses of prostitution were licensed, in effect, without regard to any law, because Butte needed the money and they were considered a necessary evil. On the first of every month all the occupants of the Galena Street cribs were technically placed under arrest for maintaining a disorderly resort. Then they were released on cash bonds of $10 each. The landladies of the larger houses put up $25 for themselves and $10 for each of their women. All of these bonds were forfeited to the city in the police court the next day.

That was the way it worked in theory. In practice, the city marshal and chief of police went around and collected the money. As compensation for this additional service they were allowed 10 percent of all of the fines they reported—or all that were entered on the police blotter, in any event. In the more imposing resorts, champagne was always waiting for them and they were so royally entertained that it could take them time to complete their collections.

I was out one night with Chief Waters who, in the absence of Marshal Tebo, was visiting the high class resorts. Wine had been flowing freely and the chief was feeling exceedingly comfortable. The place we visited was crowded and we were shown into a rear parlor, which had a cluster of electric lights in the center of the ceiling.

"Cap, I'll bet you can't shoot those out," I suggested.

"What'll ya bet?" asked Waters. And before I could stop him, he had his gun out and was whanging away. He smashed five out of six. Though the range was short, it was good shooting, considering the chief's condition.

The bullets tore through the floor and into a bedroom and before the last one was fired there was a great disturbance upstairs. A man was up there and one of them grazed his back and all of them went too close for comfort. He hustled away from there in a great hurry, dashing down the back stairs and running off in two feet of snow.

The methods of supervising social evils were looked upon by outsiders as shameless proceedings—but it paid the cost of policing the Bad Lands and, as a rule, were well done despite the Easterners who held up their hands in holy horror at the Butte system. The city physician saw to it that there was no spread of disease. And any female who persisted in robbing hard-working miners was hounded by the cops until she left town. So, for many years, the plan worked to the satisfaction of Butte, and that was all that mattered.

In all of its physical aspects the camp was most forbidding. There was not a tree or a flower or a blade of grass within the city limits or for two or three miles around them. The thick smoke from the smelters on the flat south of the camp, heavily impregnated with arsenic and sulphur, killed

Hell With the Lid Off

every trace of vegetation within its reach. Nature's cuts and carvings in the main range of the Rockies that escaped the clutch of the gnarled fingers of the glowing furnaces were Edenistic in their arboreal beauty. But the camp itself was a barren waste of gray, decomposed granite, with brown mineral outcroppings here and there.

The camp was born with gold but built on copper. There were a few producing mines within the city limits and most of the big ones were close to the border, with their workings extending under the town. Property in the municipality itself was too valuable to be used for hoisting works, except in remote cases. So the values underlying the camp were removed through tunnels driven from the outside. All real estate in the city was sold with the mineral rights reserved.

A WASTELAND OF MUD AND POLLUTION

No one could dig on his own property beyond the depth that was necessary for a foundation for the building he proposed to erect unless, by chance, he also owned the mining claim on which his lot was located.

The architecture was nondescript and altogether unattractive, with many of the false fronts of pioneer days surviving, even on the main streets. Within the city's confines the streets ran in fairly straight lines but outside of them they ran in all directions. In Meaderville, where the largest smelters were located, and in Centerville and Walkerville, which were practically parts of the city on the north, miners' cabins were sprawled all over the hillsides, and only one who was familiar with the locality could find his way around. Wagons carrying tons of ore to the smelters and drawn by eight and ten horse teams cut deep ruts in the roads. There was no paving until the late nineties, and in the spring and fall many of the streets running up and down the hill were literally rivers of mud, which one crossed at the peril of being forever lost.

Frequently at night, in the winter, when the thin air was heaviest, with a wind from the south, the smoke from the smelters would roll up the hill and envelop the camp in a yellow vapor that produced violent fits of coughing. Often the sulphur fumes were so strong that one was obliged to hold his handkerchief over his mouth while walking about on the outside. The smoke never entered a warm room. But, except in cases of pneumonia, where they brought about a speedy demise, the poisonous gases produced no ill effects.

On the contrary, they seemed to act as cleansing and remedial agents, for with all of the squalor that prevailed in some of the foreign settlements, where no sanitary law was recognized, infectious and contagious diseases were practically unknown. There were a few people in the camp who were suffering with consumption in such an advanced stage that they could exist nowhere else. But so long as they did not venture out into the gloom they had no trouble with the smelter smoke. If it produced any effect at all it must have been beneficial, for none of the afflicted ones died from consumption.

Butte stood more than a mile in the air and with a low barometer that presaged a storm the low-hanging clouds would occasionally settle down over the camp and embrace it in thick, moist murk. Under such atmospheric conditions the smelter smoke would come piling up in full force and the two invaders produced a blackness that could be cut into slices with a knife. It was absolutely impenetrable for more than two feet. Because of the numerous visitations of this kind the street lights were hung very low, but with a combination of smoke and cloud one could stand directly under one of the arc lamps and see no trace of it. Hack drivers were forced to get out and lead their horses to avoid collisions. People who knew every foot of the main streets were compelled to open the door of a saloon and look inside to get their location and bearings. On one of these pitchy nights a man was shot down directly in front of our office, not more than four feet from the door. His murderer took one step into the blackness and was lost. Hell with the lid off was right!

This condition was largely due to heap roasting—which consisted of piling up ore and wood, in the open, and letting the poisonous gases burn themselves out in the absence of any stacks to carry them off. It was more economical in one way and more extravagant in another. But in the early nineties, after a large delegation of miners headed by Jim Brown called on the smelter people and threatened them with hanging if the offenses were repeated, things were somewhat better. The delegation carried ropes, which they would not have hesitated to use. They were very business-like in terrorizing the smeltermen. This was the nearest approach to government by Vigilantes that Butte had known, and many blessings were called down on their heads.

The most attractive thing about Butte was its people—the warmth of their natures, their frankness and honesty and their unspoiled naturalness. They didn't care a hoot, not even a tiny fraction of a hoot, who you were, where you came from or how much money you had—or what your name had been "back in the States." If they liked you they were your friends, in all of the Western meaning of that much abused term. If they didn't like you, they didn't bother with you at all. As long as you lived up to the standards of the camp, you were all right; otherwise, you were all wrong.

That mental attitude was brought home to me before I had been in Butte many months. In the office of the McDermott Hotel one evening I noticed a new arrival looking at me intently. There was something familiar about his face but I could not place him and he made no advances. Later on, as I was lounging in the lobby, Fred Wey, the proprietor, settled into a chair beside me.

"How are you feeling this evening, Mr. Chamberlain?" he inquired. Thinking he was addressing a man on the other side of him I paid no attention, until he nudged me and repeated his solicitous question. I turned around and saw he was smiling, with all the air of a man who was springing a good joke.

"What?" I asked.

"Oh, it's all right, only I just wanted you to know that I know who you are, or who you were back in the States. You used to live in Burlington, Iowa. That man over there comes from Burlington, and he has just been telling me about you. Your name there was Frank Chamberlain and you used to manage the Opera House. But it's all right," he hastened to add; "We don't care a damn about that out here. We don't care what your name used to be or what you did, as long as you keep your nose clean here. If they find out you're here and come after you we won't let 'em take you back, unless you want to go. That is, if you did anything you shouldn't have done, which is none of my business right now. The only thing is that the drinks are on you." And he got up and headed for the bar.

"Wait a minute," I said. "I'm perfectly willing to buy a drink, but let's get this thing cleared up. I did live in Burlington and Frank Chamberlain and I were good pals. But I am at least four inches taller than Frank. His legs are badly bowed while mine are straight. His hair is jet blank while mine is brown. His eyes are as black as his hair while mine are gray. Outside of that we may look something alike, though we never were mistaken for each other. Frank has a perfectly good name, but it doesn't happen to be mine."

"It's all right, I tell you," replied Fred, with a laugh that was plainly skeptical. "It doesn't make a damned bit of difference out here. Let's have that drink."

On the way to the bar I insisted that we pick up the man from Burlington, who had been observing our conversation, and I was soon able to convince him, to the full satisfaction of the boss of the inn, that I was not Frank Chamberlain. Not that it mattered, but it was just as well to have the case of mistaken identity cleared up.

Through all of its glowing years Butte was sufficient unto itself and a law unto itself. This was to a great extent due to the free and independent spirit of the sturdy old pioneers and the manner in which their habits of thought had been absorbed by the first of those who came after them.

Something of the camp's view of life, too, was attributable to its location, high up on the side of the continental divide and completely surrounded by mountain ranges towering more thousands of feet into the air. When the new arrival awakened on his first morning in town and looked around, he wondered how he got into the place, and how he would get out again. The rest of the world was somewhere beyond the hills, on the outside. Butte was inside of the barriers.

FIGHTERS AND FAKERS

The camp had its own code of morals and, after the fashion of the Vigilantes, it made its own laws. Labor statutes that ran contrary, whether federal or state, counted for nothing. Public opinion was supreme and unquestioned. One striking example of this was in the matter of prize fights. They never were spoken of as boxing matches, for that would have been a sham.

There never has been a more ironclad piece of legislation than the Montana law against prize fighting. It had been framed originally by a committee of Congress that must have hated athletics, and it had come down from territorial days. The moment two men put on gloves and stepped in a ring, they exposed themselves to its penalties, no matter what they were fighting for. Their seconds and handlers and everyone connected with the management of the affair were in the same boat. Conviction was certain if they were arrested, with a term in the penitentiary an inevitable consequence.

But Butte wanted prize fights. So it had them, regularly and often. The burlesque houses advertised them every week, but they were minor affairs, generally speaking. The important contests were held in Maguire's Opera House. One man who attended all of them was John E. Lloyd, sheriff of Silver Bow County. The fact that it was his sworn duty to enforce the law made no difference. The sheriff was born a Welshman and he considered prize fighting the greatest sport in the world. He would rather watch a good fight than attend an *eisteddfod*—a singing and poetry contest—the pride and joy of all Welshmen. At every contest he had a seat in the right hand state box as the guest of John Maguire, who owned the theater. W.Y. Pemberton, affectionately known throughout the camp as "Old Pem," Chief Justice of the Montana Supreme Court, who was another fight fan, sat with them when he was not held in restraint by his judicial duties over in Helena. The mayor of the city gladly accepted Maguire's invitation to join his party while the city marshal and the chief of police had ringside seats on the stage.

Everything went along smoothly for a time, with serious young men earnestly endeavoring to knock each other's block into the wings. There was plenty of bloodshed, everything was on the up and up, and the crowds, which packed the house to the roof, yelled themselves hoarse. Some of the contests were of sufficient rank to be reported by the newspapers. Gradually, word spread through sporting circles in the East that there was some easy money to be picked up in Butte. Pugs who could raise the railroad fare descended on the camp and introduced faking, with a prearranged division of the purse, which was large enough to whet the appetites of two hungry men. Then the trouble started—and the law stepped in with all of its might and majesty to promote honest sport and secure for the public a run for its money.

The Butte fight fans were by no means the suckers that the tenderfeet crooks had believed them to be. They had either been raised in an atmosphere of rough and tumble fighting or had lived long years in it. There were some smart local scrappers who had given them a liberal education in "the art of modified murder," as it was aptly described by an eminent sports writer. There were many among the battling enthusiasts who wanted murder, without modification, in return for the price of admission, and all of them wanted action. What was more, they knew when they were getting it, and they were quick to detect the first sign of a fake. The square deal headed their list of commandments and they insisted that it be lived up to.

Hell With the Lid Off

The first match between the so-called fighters from the East gave early indications of degenerating into what would be spoken of today as a necking party. The two pugs and their handlers had talked volubly about "settling an old grudge." But they showed a disposition to kiss each other as soon as they stepped in the ring. The crowd howled and the sheriff growled a warning from his box that if the two men didn't drop their affectionate attitude toward each other and get down to business he would "pinch the whole damned outfit." The referee advised the boxers as to the identity of the loud speaker and warned them of the consequences in the event that he did arrest them. The contest proceeded with more activity, though it was far from anything to brag about as a fight.

That incident gave the crowd a bright idea. Thereafter, at the first indication of faking, the spectators would call loudly for "Lloyd, LLOYD." The sheriff had a keen sense of dramatic values. He would wait until the demand became vociferous enough to suit any star performer. Then, when the contestants went to their corners at the sound of the bell, he would step over the railing of his box, stamp across the stage with the aid of the heavy cane he always carried, climb through the ropes and take his position in the center of the ring. After the applause had subsided sufficiently so that he could be heard he would say:

"You all know me. I am John E. Lloyd, Sheriff of Silver Bow County. You all know the Montana law against prize fighting," he would say with an angry glare at the men in the two corners.

"No other State has such a strict law. There is no getting away from it If I arrest you men," he would say, pointing his cane at the fighters and their seconds, "and you will go to Deer Lodge"—where the state penitentiary is located.

"Nothing can save you. And you will stay there a long while." Then he would look across the stage to the Chief Justice, who would nod approval, while the crowd shrieked its joy.

"It is my duty to enforce the law," concluded the sheriff. "But the people of Butte want prize fighting. They elected me and they should have what they want."

His voice rising, he would add: "BUT THEY WANT FIGHTING AND NOT FAKING. IF YOU GET IN AND FIGHT IT WILL BE ALRIGHT. BUT IF THERE IS ANY MORE FAKING I WILL HAVE EVERY ONE OF YOU BEHIND THE BARS IN TEN MINUTES."

With every man in the house on his feet, yelling and waving his hat, the idolized sheriff would march back to his box, with the smile of satisfaction that comes from a duty well performed. There was never anything to complain of in the action that followed his warning. The two shivering scrappers would get in and fight as though their lives depended on it, instead of a stake that was to be split evenly between them. There was enough blood to suit the most exacting devotee of the game and everyone was happy. Everybody, that is, except the two pugs, who had been forced to better each other with unseemly brutality under the threat of Butte justice.

Three or four incidents of that kind gave the faking fighters acute cases of mental and physical indigestion and they sorrowfully returned to the East, where there were easier pickings, leaving the rough mining camp, with its rough and rowdyish ways and its awesome sheriff, to men who were willing to fight.

ON SATURDAY NIGHTS, GRINDSTONES ROLLING DOWN MAIN STREET

The law against storing dynamite within the confines of the town and killing people wholesale wasn't the only regulation that the camp violated. Not by any manner of means. The ordinance against disturbing the peace and placing other lives in jeopardy was another one that was sniffed at, like the one against carrying concealed weapons. Every man in the camp who wanted to carry a gun did so, and only tenderfeet were arrested for violating the law prohibiting concealed

Hell With the Lid Off

weapons, and then only in the fear that they might lose their tempers and do harm to a native.

Infractions of the law involving the peace and quiet generally took place about midnight or soon after on Saturday nights. Sidewalks on the two blocks along Main Street between Broadway and Galena, in front of the gambling houses and the Comique Theater, were more densely packed then than at any other time in the week—except Sunday nights. Then the whole street was alive with people.

Wild whoops from upper Main Street were the starting signal. Old-timers cocked their ears for a second to catch the tones from the babel of sound all around them. Then, identifying a gladsome pitch in the racket, they, too, let out yells and plunged headlong into side streets and open doorways, with new-timers in close pursuit. The latter did not know what it was all about. But they had sense enough to recognize that when the people of the camp took to their heels, it was wise to follow suit. Street cars on Broadway and Park Streets stopped at the near corner and hack drivers looked up the hill apprehensively, at the same time getting their steeds under control.

In five or six seconds the cause of the scramble was made apparent, when a big grindstone hurtled down the street, headed for South Butte or some point in between. Often it stayed in the middle of the road, for there was no paving in those days and it followed the car tracks on which it was started, ending its mad career in the old placer diggings below the city. Sometimes it hopped up on the sidewalk, in which case there would be a wild rush for cover, and occasionally it tore into the front of a store. The next day, damage was made good by the playboys.

The street railway to Centerville and Walkerville was then a cable road, and one grindstone went right through a train that was standing, fortunately empty, at the end of the line between Park and Galena Streets. It wrecked the grip car but did little damage to the trailer, entering by the front door and leaving by the rear, and, with its speed practically unchecked, continued on its way south. That loss, too, was promptly made good. Luckily, no pedestrian or vehicle was ever hit, though there were some narrow escapes.

Rolling grindstones down the hill was a favorite amusement of Lee Mantle, who would become a U.S. senator, grocer P.J. Brophy, his partner George Casey, John Caplice and their friends. It was made easy by the location of Caplice & Co., with its general merchandise, and afterward the Tuttle Hardware. There were always plenty of grindstones out in front and, as they were too big and heavy to be moved easily, they were left out all night. Butte was built on a side hill, which was a constant temptation to the rolling game, and the descent from Quartz Street to Granite was quite steep. From there the grade was easier, but still sufficient to increase the speed of a racing grindstone.

When the gang got about so-so in the course of their weekly revels they were moved by a common impulse to saunter, or stagger, up Main Street and attack the grindstones. They would pick out the biggest one they could handle, take it out to the middle of the street and, with a mighty shove, start it off down the hill, regardless of who was in its path or whom it might hit, wishing it well with a series of yells. Sometimes, if they were in just the right mood, they would send two or three on a mad career. Then they would saunter, or stagger, down the hill to Ernest Lange's or some other favored saloon.

Those yells, it must be conceded, were the salvation of many lives, for they were properly interpreted as a warning to everyone to get out of the way. And, like every warning in Butte, this one was shown every mark of respect. Some of the grindstones were discovered the next day, or the day after, but some of them were picked up, in a wheelbarrow or wagon, by men who needed one, or thought they did. The hardware company could not have made much money on grindstones. The police did not interfere, except to get the people out of the way, for it was recognized that the boys were just enjoying themselves, and no one was injured. So the game was continued until the camp began to put on some metropolitan airs.

These weekly disturbances were a part of the life of the camp. Butte saw all things clearly and it recognized that Saturday night was the time for play, with all of the next day in which to sober up. Every night was play night, so far as that was concerned, but Saturday and Sunday nights were the gayest and most festive occasion. Two or three, or half a dozen, members of a clique might get together on any other night, and often did. But if a man did not show up on a couple of Saturday nights in succession, it was assumed that he did not have the money to spend and his credit was openly questioned, with offers of help from many sources.

This was, almost literally, one of the camp's unwritten laws. P.J. Brophy, one of the leading fun-makers of the Casey gang, and a leading wholesale and retail grocery man, suddenly married and reformed. He abandoned his rough and rowdy ways completely and retired to enjoy the companionship of his wife. The other members of the crowd could not understand how marriage could have such a pronounced effect on a man. They debated the question at length, and it was all of six months before Brophy's credit was fully reestablished—which showed that the camp was just about as serious with its pleasures as it was with business.

That was Butte's way. What it had it hung onto, and what it wanted it got.

The Anaconda Standard

ANACONDA, MONTANA, SATURDAY MORNING, JUNE 30, 1894.

KEEPS GROWING

The Strike Hourly Becomes Greater.

MANY MORE ROADS IDLE

The End Is Apparently a Long Way Off.

GREAT LOSS IS RESULTING

The Contest Has Now Extended to Nearly Every Road West of Chicago—The Northern Pacific and Southern Pacific Paralyzed—Unsuccessful Attempts to Move Trains—A. R. U. Men at Omaha Refuse to Comply With President Debs' Orders to Strike—At Chicago the Stock Yards and Packing Houses Are Heavy Sufferers—Railroad Managers Say There Will Positively Be No Compromise—Talk of Arresting President Debs—There May Be a Strike on the Montana Union.

BUTTE, June 29.—Definite steps to prevent the running of any more Pullman cars out of Butte were taken at a special meeting of the A. R. U. to-night. The meeting was very brief and everything was short and to the point. It was decided by an unanimous vote that if the Union Pacific runs a Pullman into Butte to-morrow the Montana Union tracks the employes of the latter company will strike to a body.

As the Union Pacific uses the Montana Union tracks from Silver Bow to Butte it is believed that this decision will prevent any more Pullmans from being brought to Butte. If the cars come in, however, the men say that they will never go out till the boycott is removed. It is altogether probable that, unless the Union Pacific abandons the use of Pullman cars from the Utah & Northern, the line from Butte to Ogden will be tied up in a hard knot and the ends tucked under, by them. President Calderhead received the following this evening from W. E. Downey, President of the A. R. U. lodge at Lima:

We meet to-night to act on Debs' strike message. Wire quick your action, so that we can together.

Mr. Calderhead wired the Lima lodge immediately after the close of to-night's meeting telling them what had been done and it is expected that they will follow suit.

The A. R. U. men at Lima take the ac-

AT LIVINGSTON.

One Man Hauled Over the Coals and Exonerated at Last.

Special Dispatch to the Standard.

LIVINGSTON, June 29.—Although there are quite a number of Northern Pacific employes in this city, especially within the ranks of the Brotherhood of Locomotive Engineers, who are not members of the A. R. U., their sympathies are with the union in this, the greatest railroad strike in the history of this country. While the engineers, as a body, may not be in perfect accord with the strike, yet they will take no action calculated to interfere in any manner with the success of the strike movement.

As the engineers have not yet gone out, the strikers' committee in this city arranged for a conference with a committee of engineers this afternoon. It being a secret conference, nothing could be learned with regard to the meeting, more than that the engineers declared themselves to be in sympathy with the A. R. U. in their fight with organized capital.

This morning Night Dispatcher Elliott refused to perform a certain piece of work assigned him by Chief Dispatcher McCune, the work in question consisting in performing the duties devolving upon operators. Mr. Elliott was immediately told that he could take a lay off. This evening, however, he was sent for by Superintendent Finn and told that he could go to work notwithstanding the fact that he still refused to take the work of operators. This illustrates the feeling all the dispatchers entertain of the strike. They are willing to do dispatchers' work but they won't perform the duties of the striking operators.

The stranded passengers are being provided with meals and sleeping quarters by the company free of charge, these arrangements having been made this morning. The National Park Transportation company has put on a line of stage coaches between this city and Helena. Two four horse Concord coaches, loaded with 20 stranded passengers, left this afternoon for Helena and will make the run in 48 hours.

At a meeting of the strikers' executive committee, arrangements were made for taking care of a number of stranded passengers riding on passes, and whom the company refused to supply with meals. Cow Coroner Williams, who arrived here to-night from Helena on a handcar, was given permission by the strikers to continue his journey to Glendive.

The populist club of Livingston, composed largely of A. R. U. men, held a special meeting to consider the action of the president, E. Phinney, in declining to quit work in Master Mechanic Brown's office and join the strikers. A committee was appointed to wait on the gentleman and inform him that, as president of the club, his action had caused grave doubts in the minds of the members as to his loyalty to the club and friendship for the laboring classes.

Mr. Phinney appeared and explained his reasons for not joining the strikers. He said he had not taken the place of any

Patterson's car was attached. The engine crew switched the cars on the side track and it was the only train which moved here since the strike began. Belated travelers are going overland by private conveyances to Fort Buford to take the Great Northern to points east and west. The mails from here have been sent the same route on the weekly stage line.

A small daily paper called the A. R. U. Striker is being issued by the Independent Publishing company, with associated press dispatches. It keeps the men posted on what is going on in the different parts of the country.

Eight train crews, one passenger and seven freight, from the Missouri division, whose homes are in Dickinson and Mandan, are tied up here.

GREAT LOSS RESULTING.

Packing Houses in Chicago Suffering Immense Damage.

CHICAGO, June 29.—The packers at the stock yards tried to induce the strikers to take eight train loads of beef held by them through, as the refusal to do so would result in throwing thousands of men at the yards out of employment. The men refused and the trains were returned to the packing houses. The packers say they will be afraid to send perishable freight out of the yards while the strike continues.

As a result, business at the stock yards will be tied up whether the employes in the yards strike or not.

To-day two trains of live stock on the Santa Fe and Illinois Central outside of the yards remained on the tracks because the trainmen refused to move them.

The Chicago & Alton is badly crippled. Freight traffic is badly congested and much perishable goods is being ruined. The A. R. U. officials claim they will have the road tied completely up.

President Debs says that within 24 hours matters will so shape themselves that the strike on the Burlington would be effective. Said Debbs: "It is life or death with one of the two sides. We must kill the managers soon, or it must disrupt organized labor for years to come."

It was reported to-day in connection with the general managers' conference that plans had been formulated for the arrest, on charges of conspiracy, of Debs and Organizer Lynch. It was said the general managers had been advised to arrest these men and have them searched for papers that, if found, would furnish indisputable evidence that certain men were amenable to the conspiracy law.

The Milwaukee & St. Paul railroad shops at Milwaukee were shut down today on an order received from the general offices of the company in this city. Fifteen hundred men are thrown out of employment.

The following circular was distributed this afternoon:

To the employes of the Chicago & Northwestern: The effort now being made by irresponsible persons to induce the employes of the company to abandon employment with the avowed object of crippling this company in the discharge of its duty as a common carrier should meet with no favor whatever. There is no grievance between this company and

ALWAYS AHEAD

Enterprise Makes the Hills of Mount...

NEWS AS SHE'S P...

In the Matter of Getting the "Standard" Makes the...

OVER THE HILL BY H...

People on the Tied Up Montana Can't Do Without Favorite Newspaper Don't Have To—Th... Brought Regret to M... This Newspaper's Spee... of Hand Cars Pack a Gladness Into Many C... Camps.

BUTTE, June 29.—A special Butte at 7:45 o'clock this morning the Northern Pacific line for Livingston and Billings. Th... not have any Pullman car a... consisted of three handcars with three days' STANDARDS Eastern Montana. The strik... the people in that part of th... out any definite news of the newspapers have reached the strike began, and all the they have had has been a few telegrams.

So the STANDARD made a... to cover its field in Eastern usual. The hard pull for the up the mountain from the Homestake tunnel, a distance This was covered in one hour minutes, and then it was down to Bozeman.

At Homestake the people d... what had happened until the were placed in their hands. trains had stopped running l... suspect that there was a strike but they did not know what it The STANDARD train for East... will leave Butte at 7 o'clock ing until the strike is over.

A similar system was inau... day to take the STANDARDS Montana. The papers were t... rison by the Montana Union there taken by railroad velocipede soula. This train will also le...

All of which goes to show want the news you must tak... ARD, and if you take the ST...

CHAPTER 5
A NEWSPAPER TAKES ROOT

How not to impress your editors

Egg put the two-column headline in big black letters - W.A. CLARK'S BALLS - over a dispatch from New York about Clark's social hilarities

A man of Chinese heritage was a witness in a civil suit in the district court in Butte and there was some difficulty in making him understand the nature and value of an oath. Finally a lawyer inquired if he knew about Jesus Christ.

His face lit up and his eyes sparkled. "Sure," he replied. "Him name Markee Da-lee."

That settled the matter to the satisfaction of the court and there was a pretty general feeling throughout the camp that the disciple of Confucius had come fairly close to telling the truth. For, first of all and above all, Marcus Daly was loyal to his friends, most of whom were miners when his early day friendships were formed. Next to that— or perhaps along with it, for you show me a man whose friends can do no wrong and I will show you a man whose enemies can do no right—he was stubborn; as stubborn as only a red-blooded Irishman can be. It would be easier to move a hill of solid granite than to move Daly when his mind was made up, and quickness of decision was one of his strong points.

He was, "at every mark in the road," a builder—big and broad and unbelievably generous. He had visions, and he lived to realize them, though not to fully enjoy them. But he found enjoyment enough to satisfy any ordinary man, which he distinctively was not, in the companionship of his friends and in keeping W.A. Clark out of the United States Senate. And he was the greatest man who ever owned a newspaper, and gloried in it; there was always a question in my mind as to whether he was not prouder of The Anaconda Standard than he was of his mines, and I am sure he was, in proportion to the investment.

A $4,000 colt was responsible for the Standard. Daly had heard of J.H. Durston, of the Syracuse, N.Y., Standard and concluded that he was the man he wanted when he decided to have a paper of his own. So he sent for him to come out and look the ground over. Durston saw all of Anaconda in 10 minutes and said no. He could not see how a town could ever grow enough to support a newspaper of any size—and he was strong for a big town paper.

"But it won't be just an Anaconda newspaper," explained Daly, "It will be published here but its chief circulation will be in Butte, where Clark has the Associated Press franchise. Go up to Butte and look the camp over and then let me know. I will send the papers up there every morning on a special train in time to be delivered at the same hour as the Miner."

So Durston went to Butte, and remained of the same opinion. But just before he met Daly, to give him his final decision, he heard that he had paid $4,000 for a colt.

"Well, what is your opinion now?" asked Daly.

"I hear you've bought a colt for which you paid $4,000," replied Durston. "Is it true?"

"Yes. I think he will make a racehorse. His breeding makes him worth a bet anyway."

Hell With the Lid Off

"Well, if you're the man who pays $4,000 for an untried colt," said Durston "I guess you're the man who can put 10 times that, and as much more as may be needed, into a newspaper. I'll go you."

NEWS SANS
"NODS, WINKS OR PRODS FROM ANYBODY"

Durston sent to the Syracuse Standard for C.H. Eggleston, as his assistant, and W.W. Walsworth to be manager of the Butte office, and a force was organized, with Alex. Devine as business manager and John R. Walkup as superintendent of the composing room. And the Standard was launched in a well-equipped building in Anaconda. Money was not wasted under the thrifty Durston, but neither was any effort made to save money. A special wire was strung from the Butte office to the Standard office in Anaconda with our own operators at both ends, and nothing that was needed to make it a success was neglected or overlooked.

The paper was going great guns when I arrived in the camp. It was essentially a Butte newspaper and it had more circulation than the Miner in those days. Soon it had twice as much, then three times and after we threw the fear of the Lord into them after the big dynamite explosion it had four times as much, or more. It took the full Associated Press service and was the best newspaper published between St. Paul and the Pacific coast. At one time it had more typesetting machines than any other paper in the country except one in New York. I had the police run and also took charge of sporting events, and did other things when I wasn't busy. Which kept me fairly well occupied. There were two or three other reporters, besides Wally, who, when occasion demanded, could write like a house afire. And it is the truth to say that there was no black list, nor any kind of a blue list on the paper. We got the news and wrote it about as we pleased, without nods or winds or prods from anybody. But we tried to get ALL the news.

Durston was dignified—exceedingly so when he was full of vermouth cocktails. He was serious, slow of speech and in his movements, but a corking good newspaperman. C.H. Eggleston, who would become the editor—Egg, we called him—said little ordinarily. But his mind was working all of the time, and he was full of quiet humor. On one occasion he put a two column headline, in big, black type—W.A. CLARK'S BALLS—over a dispatch from New York telling of some of Clark's social hilarities, and much of his stuff was widely quoted. He came up to Butte about once a month for an outing. Then it was my job to take him to the Comique or the Casino, let him pick out a girl who was to his liking, get them a box, take a drink or two with them, and then go away and forget about him until he showed up at the office. He was in the Comique the night Billy Fay practically emptied it, and it is a matter of record that he didn't change his seat. Which shows that he was nothing of a coward. When he heard of the fuss his editor, Durston, had kicked up over the affair he chuckled over it for days.

Devine was a good man, too, as business managers go, but when he had one too many he had a whiney way that caused Mr. Daly to deliver one of his epigrams, which was often quoted. He came in the office one night when Alex was whining about wanting more salary and needing more help and a lot of stuff of that kind. The Old Man listened patiently for two or three minutes. Then he said, with an air of disgust: "Hell, Alex, you can't overwork a poor man and a good man won't be overworked." Alex took that tip and quit whining.

Wally was, without question, the best city editor who ever lived! He always knew what the Old Man was doing and what he was thinking about, and he never failed to steer us right. If a man's foot slipped and he was beaten on something, which happened on rare occasions, he'd hear about it in private. On the other hand, if, as often happened, a man landed a scoop, he was complimented in public. Wally finally retired and went down to southern California, got religion, took it seriously, and died there. Peace to his ashes.

Hell With the Lid Off

At about the time pictures were playing a prominent part in the metropolitan press, we concluded we ought to have an artist. So we got one—though he played a very short engagement and never drew a picture for the Standard. His name was Kemble—not the Kemble who drew funny pictures of colored men, and kids, but another, whose first name I have forgotten. He came from New York and had never been as far West as Butte. The perfect freedom of life, and especially the open gambling and the saloons that were open 24 hours a day, Sundays included, completely fascinated him. He spent most of his time in the combination, and never ceased to wonder at the skill shown by the faro dealers in the shuffling of chips with one hand, nonchalantly, while the players were getting their bets down.

Instead of going on to Anaconda and getting his name on the payroll, he remained in the camp for several days. One night the Silver Bow Club gave its annual dinner and I was down to cover it. I was grousing around the office when Kemble heard me. He asked about the Club and I told him it was the swellest thing in Butte—and that I had been warned by Harry Carns, the steward, to go lightly on the punch, in which he had put a particularly strong "stick." That appealed to Kemble a whole lot, as well as the story that the ladies had a habit of dancing on the piano, and he allowed he would go in my place.

So he went to his room and changed his clothes and sailed away. I imagine that while he was making the shift he took on a few more than he already had, which was quite enough, but that was his own lookout, and it cost him his job, in jig time. At all events, Kemble was mauling the daylights out of the piano, in the Club's music room—and he certainly could play—when Durston came in, with his friend Captain Palmer, the president of the club. Both had about all of the vermouth cocktails they could carry well and both were very dignified.

"Who is that young man who is playing the piano?" asked Durston. "I feel that I would like to play some."

"His face looks familiar," said Palmer, who was looking at Kemble for the first time, though he saw three of him. "But I don't place him. However, we will fix that all right."

"Would you mind letting my friend Durston play a while," he said to Kemble. "You play very nicely, of course, but Mr. Durston is also an accomplished player. I am Captain Palmer, the president of the club."

"Certainly," agreed Kemble, who though not fully himself, had some of the instincts of a gentleman. And he surrendered the seat to Durston.

Durston sat down heavily, and then began laboriously to play something heavier, of the sort that was popular when he was young. He may have been able to play when he was at the University of Heidelberg, which we were often hearing about, but advancing years and vermouth cocktails so interfered with his touch that he made rather a mess of things. It was all right with Palmer, but to Kemble's ears it was just a jumble of discords. He stood it as long as he could, then to the accompaniment of "You're one hell of a player," he seized Durston by the shoulders and threw him under the piano. Palmer undertook to interfere on behalf of his friend, and Kemble accommodatingly took the same course with him.

Then he renewed his attack on the piano, while Durston crawled out from one end of the gaily resounding instrument while Palmer crawled out from the other. But Kemble was not playing when Palmer finally got to his feet. He discovered that there were limits to the freedom of the individual in the camp and that such marked discourtesy to the president of the club overstepped the mark. Consequently he was gently but firmly removed from the room by the time Durston and Palmer were in a position to make inquiries. The seemingly indignant waiters—who really did not like Palmer, who wished himself into the position of General Manager of the Butte & Boston Company and was generally regarded as a good deal of a bore, as well as a boor—identified the men he had been using as ten pins, where upon he went ahead and got good and drunk.

"Who was that very much intoxicated young man who was at the Silver Bow Club dinner tonight?" inquired Mr. Durston, very solemnly, when he came into the office a little before 3 o'clock. "He claimed to represent the Standard, but I never saw him before."

"That was Mr. Kemble, our new artist," I said.

"Hmm. He was our new artist, you mean."

And Kemble lost his job right there, without having done a day's work for the paper. He took his departure, still convinced that Butte was the most wonderful city in the world. That gave us a bad start with artists and we did not get another one as long as I stayed in the camp.

CHAPTER 6
THE SHREWDNESS OF MARCUS DALY

Checkered quests of W.A. Clark

To complainers about stories, Old Man Daly would say: "It's true I own the paper, but the boys down there won't do a darn thing I want them to"

Frequently in the afternoon, on his way to the train to Anaconda, the Old Man, by which title we all knew Mr. Daly, dropped into the office to compliment us on something we had said or done or simply for a gabfest. He was a stickily built man about 5 feet 8 inches tall, with a ruddy face and eyes that twinkled most of the time, though when he was angry they were hot fire. And when he did not speak softly it was a sure sign that he was aroused. Those afternoon sessions were a treat. Occasionally the Old Man would tell of some friend of his who had come to him about the newspaper, almost with tears in his eyes, about a flick of sarcasm or a dig at some lease being worked or something else of minor importance. To practically all complaints of this kind the Old Man made the same reply. He would listen patiently to all the man had to say, and then explain, with some show of feeling:

"Yes, it is true that I own that paper, and the funny thing is that the boys down there won't do a darn thing I want them to. There is no use of my saying anything to them. I'd just forget it, if I were you." Which was something of a joke, for there wasn't one of us who would not have jumped through the hoops for him. But there was never a word of criticism, no matter whom we hit or how hard.

The Old Man saved my bacon more than once. The first time was when City Marshal Jim McNichols and Street Commissioner Pete McArthur, with the cooperation of Mayor Dugan and Chairman Harrington, waited on him and called for my scalp. Another time was when a cage fell away in the Anaconda mine with a load of men and deposited them, in pieces, 500 feet below. The cage had been tested just a few days before by being cut loose with a load of ore, and the safety dogs worked perfectly. But they seldom worked when men were on board. I wanted to go down and look around. But Paddy Kane, the superintendent, turned me down cold, though under ordinary conditions he was genial enough. So in the story the next morning I went the limit in implying that the accident was Paddy's own fault. Paddy complained bitterly to the Old Man the next day.

"That's just what I've got that paper for," said the Old Man. "I want them to roast you when you don't do what they want you to do, within reason. That was a reasonable request Smith made, and I would have granted it if I had been you." Paddy and I got along better after that.

And when Durston whined that I was "trying to get him killed" and demanded my head on a platter when I neglected to send him menacing gambler Billy Fay's message that it was all right for him to use that story, the Old Man just laughed and laughed. There were other occasions, too, when Daly stood between me and destruction. One would have thought that, with all the multiplicity of interests in his charge, the Old Man would have been too busy to concern himself with a youngster of a reporter and that the second request, at least, would have landed me. But that was Marcus Daly.

Hell With the Lid Off

In a burst of enthusiasm I once ran a personally conducted tour in a handcar, loaded with newspapers, from Butte to Bozeman, a distance of 95 miles, and the effort nearly cost my life. It was during the American Railway Union strike, which tied up the transcontinental lines in Montana tighter than a drum. After it had dragged along for about a week the people were clamoring for news and it occurred to me that it would be a bright idea to deliver papers via handcar as far as Bozeman, at any rate. The strikers, having nothing else to do, I believed, would be glad to take the handcar over to their sections. All I would have to do would be to ride and boss the job. The notion was so brilliant that it almost scintillated.

I took the matter up with J.W. Naugle, the chairman of the striking employees, and he had the same idea. Instructions were issued accordingly—but, very unfortunately, no date was set. For once my luck was bad, for we hit on a day when American Railway Union meetings were held all along the line, outside of Butte. The car was loaded with as many papers as it would carry, and still leave room for the men to pump, and we set forth in gay spirits bright and early one morning I joined the pumpers at the start, for it was a sharp upgrade for six or seven miles to the crest of the mountains To our great surprise there was no relief crew waiting for us there. We supposed, however, that they had been detained a little and, as it was downgrade for quite a ways from there, I set out bravely all alone.

I discovered why there were no men in sight at the first station, but, being naturally sort of bull-headed, I determined to continue on the way, all alone—and I felt more alone every minute. Pumping a handcar is hard work for one who is accustomed to it, and for a man who is used to no harder work than pushing a pencil it is torture. At Manhattan— strangely enough—a flag station about eight miles west of Boseman, I ran upon the first man I had seen since leaving Butte. He was a bow-legged cowboy, who knew nothing more about a handcar than I did but I employed him to help me with the last stretch—I would have engaged him if he had had only one arm and no legs. A big crowd met the "Standard Special" in Bozeman. But I entirely missed the thrill of it and lost all interest in the proceedings until I had slept the clock around.

After I regained my senses, and some of my strength, the men took us back, all right—as it had been promised they would take me over. But on the return trip I was only a passenger. Mr. Daly was annoyed about that experience; if we had only told him what we planned to do he would have sent along a crew of husky miners to do the pumping. But such is life in the far West!

It was his devotion to his friends—his complete understanding of the exactness with which the Old West defined the much-abused word "friendship"—that accounted for Daly's marvelous popularity. But his friendship was so natural and his generosity so unrestrained that by no stretch of the imagination could it be attributed to selfishness. His pocketbook was always open and no man in need appealed to him in vain. His old friends from Virginia City, Nevada, called on him by the score, and all of them were put to work. If they were too old to work underground they were given jobs as watchmen, and if they were very old they were set to work watching rocks that were firmly embedded in the decomposed granite of the Anaconda hill, to see that they did not work loose and roll down on Dublin Gulch. When his old friends died their widows called and left their savings with him for investment. He would put their money in his safe, and in a few weeks give them two or three times the amount they had left with him. He established schools and hospitals without any regard to race or creed.

One case will do as an illustration. Dennis Nevin, who had worked with Daly in Virginia City, Nevada, in the early 60s, arrived in Butte about the same time Daly did and later on was given a job in the Wake-Up-Jim mine, when it was a bucket mine. The rope broke and Nevin was killed. Daly promptly built two big boarding houses for the widow and helped her financially until she was on her feet. One son, Joe, was made foreman of the Mountain Con mine and another, Chas. P., was elected mayor of Butte. Does anyone suppose there was any way of getting those men away from Daly? And the camp was spotted with men who were more or less in the same boat, and they all had their friends.

With his old cronies from the Comstock mines he was lavishly generous. Miles Finlen—the man for whom the best hotel in Butte is named, his son having given the ground on which it stands—made a fortune from one lease alone and could have had as many more as he wanted. Pat Mullins was another who learned to walk on velvet. Pat made himself famous as mayor of Butte by introducing President Theodore Roosevelt as the hero of San Juan Hill and by his command to the waiters at Roosevelt's banquet: "Bring on the food." There were many others in the same class, and Mr. Daly was always just the same as he had been when they were working together in Virginia City.

'LIKE A GIANT ANACONDA'

Daly was born in 1841, the son of comfortable farmers in County Cavan, Ireland who were known throughout the countryside as horse breeders and trainers. Some of their blood was passed on to Daly. His ancestors were princes of Corea Adaim in Westmeath for 2,000 years. There were 10 other children and when he was 15 he left school and set sail for New York, alone. His first job was delivering messages for a telegraph company; then he was employed as a dock laborer. He saved his money and when he was 20 he bought a ticket for California. There he worked as a farm hand until he met Thomas Murray—later on superintendent of the Anaconda smelter yard until he died—who persuaded Daly to accompany him to Calaveras County in search of a mining job.

Daly was then on the trail which he never lost. When they lined up to apply for work, the bully of the camp was nearby and, seeing Daly and Murray, he weighed in with an insulting remark about "greenhorn Irish." Marcus promptly knocked him down, and out, with a smash to the chin.

Hell With the Lid Off

This so pleased the foreman that he at once employed both Marcus and Thomas, and they stayed there four years, living in a log cabin and cooking their own food. Then they moved to Virginia City, Nevada, at that time the greatest silver mining camp in the world, and went to work in the Comstock. Daly made a quiet study of geology, and by 1870 his reputation as a mining man and one who could "see into the ground" farther than most men had spread to Utah, and he was engaged to take charge of the Ophir mine. His success was such that the Walker Brothers, mining men and bankers of Salt Lake City who owned the Ophir, in 1876, sent him to Walkerville, just north of Butte, to examine the Alice mine, and buy it if he thought well of it. He purchased it for $5,000, retaining a one-fifth interest for himself, which he sold a year later for $30,000.

He then looked over the Butte Hill, about which he had been dreaming dreams. There he found that two other Irishmen, Michael and Edward Hickey, owned a mine which they had located with Charles X. Larrabee, and that they wanted to sell because they did not have enough money to develop it. They had a shaft down about 75 feet on a well-defined silver vein. Michael Hickey had named the claim Anaconda because, as a soldier in the Union Army, he had read one of Horace Greeley's editorials in which he said that McClellan was enveloping Lee's Army "like a giant anaconda." And the name stuck in his mind. Daly listened to their talk about the returns from silver, but it was copper he was thinking about, though no one else in the camp gave copper a thought.

Daly bought the claim for $10,000, and the great Anaconda Copper Mining Company was born. He went to California and interested capitalists George Hearst and J.B. Haggin, who had become wealthy in mining and both of whom he had known on the Comstock. Then Daly went after the copper he knew was there—and proved his right to be called the "Copper King." When Hearst and Haggin threw up their hands and quit after Daly threw silver ore on the dump, without assaying it, he went on and developed the Anaconda with his own money. And he was almost at the bottom of his pocket when, at the 300 foot level, they cut a five-foot vein of copper glance which ran 30 percent copper, and grew richer and bigger with increased depth.

Hearst and Haggin came in again then, and the busy days for Daly began. He bought all of the adjoining properties at bargain prices before his secret leaked out. The nearest smelter that could handle sulphide copper was in Swansea, Wales, and the nearest railroad was 100 miles away, but getting closer every day. In the wilderness 26 miles from Butte, Daly built the town of Anaconda, and the greatest copper smelter in the world, with plenty of water. And, profiting by the experience of Butte, he built immense flues and great stacks at the top of the hills, so that all of the destructive smoke, which lost much of its elements in the flues, was carried over the town and vegetation was not interfered with at all. And when the flues were cleaned out once a year enough gold and silver and arsenic and sulphur were found to pay for them.

The smelter was finished in 1883—and Hearst and Haggin presented Daly with a check for $100,000. He brought furnace men from Wales and mill men from northern Michigan to train the young Americans who were under them. He bought immense tracts of virgin forests to furnish the mines with timber. He bought coal and iron and silica properties and established in Anaconda the Steel and Iron Foundry. He founded coal mining towns in Belt, Montana and Diamondville, Wyoming and in Anaconda built the Montana Hotel, then the finest in the Northwest, and the Margaret Theater, then the largest in the state.

In addition to the Standard, he built the Butte and Anaconda race tracks, the latter Eden-like in its surroundings. He backed the Butte football team, built the Anaconda water works and electric light plant and, in Butte, the Florence Hotel, with ideal accommodations for nearly 650 miners—to mention a few of his successes. In 1895, the Montana Union railway refused to make a lower rate on the ore it was hauling to Anaconda from the bins of a dozen mines. So Daly built the Butte, Anaconda & Pacific Railway, a short-line running from Anaconda to Butte.

W.H. Burns was general manager of the Montana Union, which was owned jointly by the Northern Pacific and Union Pacific. He pleaded in vain for the lower rates which Mr. Daly wanted.

"Mr. Daly says he will build his own road if we don't come down," he told the owners.

"He's not going to build any railroad in these times," they said, complacently.

"You don't know Marcus Daly," Burns told them.

At daylight on the morning the time for them to relent expired, Daly put thousands of men at work all along the line and the road was rushed through.

Daly bought 22,000 acres of land in the beautiful Bitter Root Valley, 150 miles west of Butte, where he built a handsome country home and a breeding farm that was as fine as it could be made, where he relaxed and rejoiced. There was an open track for summer and a covered one for winter, all of the roads were graveled and lined with trees. The establishment looked like a small town. There lived Tammany, one of the greatest winners of the era.

In a match race in New Jersey, Tammany beat the acclaimed Lamplighter by four lengths for $40,000, on which Daly was credited with winning $250,000. Tammany also was winner of: the Lawrence Realization; the Eclipse Stakes; the Jerome Stakes; the Withers Stakes; and the Lorillard Stakes. He was Horse of the Year nationally in 1892. Daly's stable was sold at auction at Madison Square Gardens after his death and brought $732,328. If he had lived a few years longer, Daly would have had, along with thoroughbreds Hamburg, Sysonby and Inflexible, the greatest stallions in the United States and a corner on every race horse in America.

In 1872 Daly was married in Salt Lake City to Miss Margaret Evans, a school teacher. She was a Presbyterian and he was a Roman Catholic. He had four children:

his son, Marcus II, who dropped dead while hunting in Virginia; and his daughters, Margaret Augusta Daly; Mary Daly Gerrard; and Harriott Daly.

Daly died of Bright's disease, a kidney ailment, at the Hotel Netherland in New York on Nov. 12th 1900, just as he was preparing to return to Montana. At age 58, a royal soul passed on.

Shortly before his death, Daly sold Anaconda Company to the Amalgamated Copper Company for $39,000,000. In 1907, Butte citizens erected a bronze statue of him in front of the federal building in Butte. It was the work of Augustus Saint-Gaudens, whose art embodied ideals of the American Renaissance.

Daly enjoyed politics as much as any Irishman would and played at it systematically. He controlled the city administrations of Butte and Anaconda, as a rule, and he had a large hand in state affairs. He would never accept any office, but he liked to see his friends, who had a flair for that sort of thing, realize their ambitions. He gave Democrat William Jennings Bryan, who ran three times for president starting in 1896, $250,000 for the campaign. That was one bet he lost.

But in the early days, he was one of the Big Four who controlled Democratic politics in the Montana Territory. The others: former Governor Samuel T. Hauser; Charles A. Broadwater, the banking and real estate magnate; and William A. Clark, a wealthy fellow Copper King and owner of the rival Butte Miner newspaper, a tool he used in his craving for a U.S. Senate seat.

SCANDALS OF A MAN WHO DIDN'T MEASURE UP

William Andrews Clark Sr. was a dapper dresser, a man who did all of his business from his office. Unlike Daly, he never mixed with his men. He was born in Pennsylvania of Irish parents and taught school and studied law in Missouri. After going West in the early days well in advance of Daly, he did smart trading with the bullwhackers and put himself on a course to become one of America's richest men. He became a banker in Deer Lodge before he transferred operations to Butte, in partnership with his younger brother, J. Ross Clark, who spent most of his time in Los Angeles.

Jealous of Daly's popularity, Clark could not resist the temptation to knock him. He wrote a letter to the Walker Brothers of Salt Lake—who had wisely sent Daly to Montana in the first place—alleging that Daly's management of the Alice Mine was unbusinesslike and extravagant. They paid no heed, but turned the letter over to Daly. Clark sent a similar letter to Hearst and Haggin later, with the same result. Daly smiled to himself, and said nothing.

Clark first ran for office in 1888 as the Democratic candidate for Montana's congressional delegate. It was predicted that he would have a walk-over—but Thomas H. Carter, his Republican opponent, won by 5,000 majority. Daly had quietly dropped a hint and his followers voted for Carter.

The war was on.

In 1889, Montana was admitted as a state, which Clark saw as his path to a seat in the U.S. Senate with legislatures choosing senators at the time. His maneuvering became a scandal when it was disclosed that he bribed legislators for their votes. Clark is supposed to have said: "I never bought a man who wasn't for sale."

The Democrats sent Clark and Martin Maginniss to Washington; the Republicans sent Wilbur F. Sanders, the former prosecutor of the Vigilantes, and T.C. Power. The Senate seated Sanders and Power.

Clark then made repeated efforts toward his ambition, but they were unsuccessful. In the Senate campaign of 1893, Samuel T. Hauser withdrew in favor of Clark in return for Clark's solemn promise to support Helena for the permanent capital. Instead, Clark spent a year in a foolish attempt to win Daly's support in exchange for his support of Anaconda as the capital.

A month before the election Clark threw his support, which was trifling, and the support of his money, which was much more important, to Helena, and Helena won—by 1,400 in a vote of 50,000. On the last day of the legislature that year, at the final meeting of the joint session, Clark sat in front of the speaker's desk with his speech of acceptance in his hand and a smile on his face. But it was characteristic of him that he had not bought enough votes. He was three shy, so the smile was wiped from his face and the carefully prepared speech was not delivered.

In the election of 1895 every Clark candidate was defeated. In the campaign of 1898, Clark temporarily forgot his love of money long enough to throw off all of the brakes. He corrupted the legislature shamelessly buying votes. His son, Charles W. Clark, said at the beginning of the session: "We are going to send the old man to the Senate or the poorhouse." So freely was the money passed around that there was a scarcity of $10,000 bills.

John Ball Wellcome, one of his attorneys, was disbarred in the affair and his partner, Frank E. Corbett, died from work and worry. Wellcome had said: "Every man who votes for Clark is to be paid, and the man who votes for him without being paid is a fool." He stated that W.A. Clark had ordered them to go in and win, regardless of what it cost.

On Jan. 10, state Senator Fred Whiteside arose and turned over to the speaker $30,000, which he said had been paid for three votes of men who could not be tampered with but had consented to play a part in the interests of justice. The legislature responded by unseating the honest young Whiteside. On Jan. 28th Clark was elected with 54 votes, 43 of which was said to have cost him $432,000.

Clark made the mistake, when Whiteside turned in the $30,000, of openly charging that it was "Daly's money." But for that, he probably would have been seated, for Daly believed in settling quarrels at home. But he was not content to rest under a charge of bribery. So the fight was carried to Washington, much to the dismay and confusion of the Clark forces.

Hell With the Lid Off

The U.S. Senate Committee on Privileges and Elections made a disgraceful show of Clark by his own witnesses. He was convinced their report would be against him, so he resigned. Daly made an excellent witness and offered to throw open his books and the books of all of his companies. He said the campaign cost him $40,000.

The committee reported that Clark's election "is null and void on account of briberies, attempted briberies, and corrupt practices by his agents."

In 1990, Gov. Robert Burns Smith was enticed out of the state and in an elaborate scheme, Archibald Spriggs, the lieutenant governor and a Clark ally, appointed Clark to the Senate despite the scandal. Smith hurried back, and a hot protest was sent to the Senate revoking the appointment and reciting the circumstances under which it was made. So Clark remained out of the Senate, "preferring to wait for a vindication," which came—if it could be called a vindication—not until after Daly's death. And he was no credit to Montana while he was in the Senate.

Clark's greatest success, as a money-maker, came when he bought the open-pit copper mine, United Verde, in Arizona. After his death, his lawyers are reported to have said that his dividends from this property alone were a million dollars a month.

Clark was wrong in so many ways that his first wife, Kate Stauffer, an estimable lady, would not live in the same country with him for several years before her death in 1893. When he was in Butte, she was in Paris. And when she learned that he had started toward Europe, she crossed him on the ocean.

Mark Twain said of Clark: "He is as rotten a human being as can be found anywhere under the flag; he is a shame to the American nation, and no one has helped to send him to the Senate who did not know that his proper place was the penitentiary, with a ball and chain on his legs."

The Anaconda Standard.

ANACONDA, MONTANA, SUNDAY, OCTOBER 28, 1900.

THE BOSS BOODLER IS HANDY AT IT.

CHAPTER 7
A CAPITOL RUCKUS

From covering politics to playing in the political game

'I did not eat in a union restaurant for two or three weeks, for fear of having to try to digest ground glass'

The fight between Helena and Anaconda to be the permanent capital of Montana ended, as it probably should have ended, but only by a margin of 1,400 votes out of 50,000 that were cast. Mr. Daly had his heart so strongly set on making Anaconda the capital that it was about the most bitter struggle the West ever knew. But he was even more determined to keep Clark out of the Senate. Had he been content to have him go there, the capital election might have turned out differently. But he wasn't, and he won a series of sure bets while losing one doubtful one.

At that, at this late date, it might as well be admitted that Helena won because she was entitled to win. Helena has nothing but the capital and a lot of memories of Last Chance Gulch and the placer mines, while Anaconda has the greatest copper smelter in the world, a beautiful location and a lot of memories that are more recent than those of the early days.

In 1893, and declaring openly for Helena, Clark spent nearly a year in a silly attempt to patch up his feud with Daly.

It was not until a month before the election that he threw his money, which counted greatly in the purchase of votes, and his influence, which was trifling, to Helena, greatly to the delight of the people of that very anxious city.

The constitutional convention decided that there should be a run-off election in 1892 and then, if no city received a majority, a final election in 1894 between the two top cities. Practically every city in the State entered the first race. Even Butte went in, though it did not want the capital and was quite satisfied with things as they were. One reason was that the capital was where they made the laws while Butte was the place where they openly violated all of the statutes that ran contrary to public opinion—and violation of any state law was easier away from the capital than in it. Another reason was that the capital was usually considered a dead town, while Butte was very much alive. So, altogether, public sentiment was strongly against Butte for the capital.

Besides, Mr. Daly had backed Anaconda so strongly that it was bound to run second to Helena in the general scramble, which it did. The fight in 1894 was ferocious and long drawn out. The Helena press once announced that every man who was for Anaconda wore a copper collar. We seized on that, and had badges made of squares of copper which all of the Anaconda boosters wore in the lapels of their coats—and that, by the way was the only badge I have ever worn. When press badges were needed, in Chicago, I displayed mine in my hat, where it could be easily seen and would not be in the way.

On election day, E.H. Sherman, the undertaker, and I were assigned to a ward in the heart of the city, in which practically all of the Cooks and Waiters Union—commonly known as the Hashers—lived and voted. Fortunately, there were a great many voters from the Anaconda hill living there, too. The Hashers were making good money, for Butte was then, as it is today, emphatically a union town. We could have bought the votes we needed, easily enough, for we had plenty of money, though they demanded $25 each, which was about five times the customary rate. And we saw that we got value received for every $5.

But we were stoutly opposed to this sort of traffic; being stood up and sandbagged by men who should have been solidly for Mr. Daly went against the grain a whole lot. Besides, I thought I knew a trick worth two or three of theirs. So it was up to me to deal with the Hashers. I spoke to them at their hall and reminded them that their high wages were entirely due to Mr. Daly, who had always stood for union labor. The Boston & Montana and the Butte & Boston companies had often sought to reduce wages from $3.50 a day to $2.50 or $3, but Daly had firmly opposed any reduction.

"If a man isn't worth $3.50 a day he isn't worth anything," said Mr. Daly. As he employed more men than both of the Boston companies, the threatened reduction never came off. And all of the ages in the cap were kept up through his instrumentality.

The Cooks and Waiters said they knew of their obligation to Mr. Daly and ordinarily they stood with him, but this was an exceptional situation—which, though a poor excuse, was better than none. I knew, though I did not tell them so, that $10 was all they could get from Helena, at most. I said we would have to get instructions from many a higher-up to pay $25 a vote. And whoever it was that could issue the necessary orders wasn't at his office, and it required time to locate him, and all the rest of it, so it was after 4 o'clock when I finally threw up my hands and told them to go ahead and vote. Then they rushed for the booth.

In the meantime we had sidetracked every man from the hill that we were sure of and held them in reserve, to which they consented readily enough when the situation was explained to them—which was not so much of a concession, in view of the fact that they had been given the day off to vote. They voted like clockwork, just the same. When the Cooks and Waiters reached the voting place they found a long line ahead of them—and the polls closed just as the last man was reached. Not a single Hasher voted, in our precinct. I was threatened with every punishment under the sun. Their threats did not worry me any, but the black looks were so numerous that I did not eat in a union restaurant for two or three weeks, for fear of having to try to digest ground glass.

Success made us confident and early in the afternoon Dave Meiklejohn, a deputy U.S. Marshal and a secret service agent for anyone who would employ him, came around to look us over. He was for Helena, of course, and it struck me that he probably would have a warrant out for us, for we made no secret of buying votes, and the less so when Davey was around. So Sherman hustled out and got a bond for $10,000 for each of us, so that we would have it ready. But Davey probably was simply looking for evidence to upset the election, if it went for Anaconda.

During the afternoon we received word that an unknown Anaconda champion in Helena had got drunk and yelled "Hurrah for Anaconda" in the main street of the town. Wherefore he was promptly mobbed and jailed. An hour later a special train left Butte with two of Daly's lawyers, a bundle of cash and a number of friends. The man was bailed out and was subsequently given a lease on ground from which he quickly cleaned up $60,000. Daly would reward men whom he did not know if they made his fight their own. Later, he cancelled the lease because the man was squandering the money.

When the votes were counted, Clark and J.M. Quinn, editor of the Miner, were telegraphed for from Helena. When they arrived they were met by a tumultuous crowd, who took the horses from their carriage and hauled them all around town. There were free drinks in all of the saloons and it was a happy day for Helena.

Geographically, perhaps Bozeman would have been a better choice, but geography had nothing to do with the capital fight. Bozeman did not particularly want it, either, but the committee there put up a good fight, just the same. One of the smartest things they did was to have a lot of coins

Hell With the Lid Off

of aluminum, which was new at the time, cast in imitation of silver dollars, with "Bozeman for the Capital" standing out on them. One of the Bozeman committee arrived in Butte in the evening with a supply of these coins and, seeing the advantage to which they could be put at the Comique theater, I appropriated a goodly part of them. These were distributed among a few good fellows, and that night was a memorable one at the Comique.

We divided ourselves up into parties and into different boxes and threw the imitation dollars on the stage, at favored performers. Two- and four-bits were quite common, especially on pay nights, but a rain of dollars, coming from different parts of the house, was sufficiently unusual to attract attention. They were quickly picked up, and the actors were canny enough to allow those who were to follow them to think they were genuine. The impression got around that a new crowd of rich Easterners had blown in, and we let it stand. The result was that before the night was over the Comique was in an uproar, which did not subside even when the joke became apparent. And quite a bunch of "new money" was put in circulation by the time it was over.

CHAPTER 8

ALL NIGHT LONG AT THEATRE COMIQUE

Bad behavior

Blow-offs at the casino

"Don't shoot the musicians; they're doing the best they can"

Theatre Comique, which was on Main Street, between Park and Galena, was one of the camp's institutions. It was comparatively new and was the best built theater in Butte. The ground floor was large and open and studded with large and small tables, at which the crowd sat and drank. There was a large, and excellent, orchestra, led by Harry Ganke who, despite the fact that he always fiddled with a cigar between his teeth, was really a fine musician. On the right-hand side, nailed to the proscenium arch, was a sign that always had the Easterners guessing as to whether or not it meant what it said:

"Don't shoot the musicians; they're doing the best they can."

The second and third floors were partitioned off into boxes, with curtains which could be dropped—and generally were—which were locked and provided the means for private parties to see without being seen, if they wished. The four boxes nearest the stage could accommodate twelve or fifteen people, and they were the exception in that the curtains were seldom down; the others were only large enough for four or six, though when a man was out for a good time they held only two. At the rear was an open space, where the girls sat when they were not engaged and regular inhabitants congregated when the boxes were all filled. There was a bar on every floor, of course, to facilitate service.

Wine was $5 a pint and the cheapest drink was beer at two-bits, on the main floor; it was $1 a bottle on the upper floors. When a party got fairly well along, the same bottle of wine was sold three or four times, to three or four; the glasses were so full of ice that they would not hold much fizz water and, when necessary, the bottle was recharged with carbonated water. Early in the morning, when general intoxication was the rule, fake liquor, which cost 16 cents a bottle, was sold in place of the real stuff.

The stage show was good, as a rule, and at times excellent. It was composed of vaudeville acts that were imported from New York, Denver and San Francisco, and was made up largely of females. In addition to their salaries, they were told that they would be expected to "work the boxes," so they arrived with full understanding. Many of the girls had never done anything of that kind, but they soon took to it and liked it. Dan Crimmins and his wife, Rosa Gore, whom old timers will remember for their vaudeville act "What are the Wild Waves Saying?" came out for a month, and were there when I left. Frank Finney came for two or three months and stayed two or three years. Lulu Watts, the girl with a diamond set in one of her front teeth, came there too, to fill an engagement, to the great distress of some of the best-known young men in the camp.

It was wild and woolly, and no mistake, people enjoyed it hugely. There was a curtain-raiser, in which about all of the members of the company appeared, a middle-act of the same kind, and along toward morning they would appear in a finale—which was well-named, from the state most of the girls were in by that time. Sometimes, with the

Hell With the Lid Off

house crowded and the waiters running around with their tongues hanging out, the middle-act was cut out entirely. In between the girls appeared on the stage and sang two songs, whether the audience wanted them or not. But usually they did, and some of them had good voices, in the first part of the show. Then they rushed back to the boxes where they were engaged.

There often were quite long waits between the acts, which were filled in by the orchestra, in galloping style. Ordinarily there was a magician, or some other male specialty, on the program, and he stayed as long as he wanted to. Dolph Levino came for a month of this work, and stayed a year or more. Ernest Hogan, of "My Gal's a Highborn Lady" fame, came out for two weeks and stayed six months.

The show began at eight and ran until three or four in the morning, and often later, and generally to a packed house. The performers worked the boxes upstairs while other girls, who made no pretense to any histrionic ability, worked the ground floor. With every round of drinks they were given checks for 20 percent of the amount of the purchase, the checks being divided among the girls who were in with the play. These were cashed in before they went home, and many of the girls added large sums to their salaries. Naturally, they all had a wine thirst all of the time, and it was generously acceded to, especially on the upper floors, where men literally fought with each other at times for the privilege of paying $5 for a 16-cent bottle of jiggly water.

For about two years the place was run by Fred Ritchie and Paul Davis. Davis had charge of the ground floor and the door, and Ritchie ran the upper floors and had the direction of the show. Even then they made money faster than they could spend it. All that was necessary to ensure a pleasant evening was to tell Davis that Ritchie said he was a sonnykabick.

"Vat, me Paul Davis, a sonnykabick? Not in a t'ousand years. Come mit me, I show him." Paul would throw up the safe, take out a roll of gold pieces big enough to buy drinks galore, and head for the Mercury Street palaces. And your fare was paid as long as you cared to stay.

The next quiet night Ritchie would be told of something purely imaginary that Davis had said about him, and it would be his turn to lead the procession.

"He said that, did he? The damned dirty Austrian sonnykabick. Well let's go and spend some of his money." And Ritchie would dig into the gold pile, and he always called a hack, though the distance was less than two blocks. That sort of thing continued for a year or more, and still they made money. Ritchie finally bought Davis out and became the master of his own fate.

Ritchie was a Westerner with Western ideas, and he ran the place in real Western style. He would get drunk occasionally on the days his programs came out, and then there would be fearful and wonderful things to behold, printed on colored paper and with profanity running all through them. One morning, after daylight had dawned and almost everybody had gone home, a crowd of cowboys came in and demanded liquor. They had been busy that night and everything in the house that was drinkable was exhausted. Richie explained that to the cow-punchers, but they didn't believe him.

There were a lot of bottles on the back bar, filled with bitters and that sort of thing, and they pounced on those and mixed up some of the most deadly concoctions that were ever shaken together and drank them with gusto. When that supply was exhausted, they walked solemnly out of the open space at the rear and landed in a heap on the main floor, breaking some chairs and tables but not injuring a one of them. Then they marched out of the front door in search of another place.

As a young man Ritchie had roamed around the West a good bit and once roomed with Will Bill Hickock. Bill never locked his door, Fred said, but placed a paper, in the form of an inverted cornucopia, so that it was certain to rustle at any attempt to open the door. And Bill was such a light sleeper, and had so trained himself, that he would be sitting up in bed with both guns down on the door before it could be opened a foot. That summer they had wind a plenty, and a sudden gust would rustle the paper as readily as the opening of the door. With Bill bouncing up and throwing his guns down on the door, the strain got too much for Ritchie and he moved. That experience—or some other experience about which he did not talk—taught him to have great reverence for a gun.

Ritchie eventually hit the slide and landed at the bottom. The last I saw of him, years later, he was ballyhooing for a snake charmer in San Francisco.

SIX-GUN "BLOWOFFS" AT CASINO THEATRE

The other burlesque theater was the Casino, down on Galena Street, just around the corner from Boston Charley's gambling house, and run by Jim Kenney, of Clipper Shades fame, or notoriety, whichever you please.

When I first landed in Butte, the Clipper Shades was the most notorious deadfall in the camp. It was on East Park Street, near Arizona, and was really a small hurdy-gurdy, with women entertainers, but not performers, for the men. And if the stories told to the police by men who complained of having been robbed there were half true, they were so slick and smooth that oil would not rest on them. Complaints of having been rolled were frequent, but when the police got there the waiter and the girl had both disappeared, so there seldom were any arrests, but plenty of trouble. It is only fair to Kenney to say that there were never any complaints of robberies in the Casino, and he always insisted that most of the complaints against the old Clipper Shades were unjustified.

Finally Kenney graduated, the Clipper Shades became just a saloon and the Casino Theatre was opened with a great flourish. The Casino was on the same order as the Comique, except that there were big stage boxes with the customary open space at the rear. It was of somewhat rough construction, and the second floor was supported by 12-by-12 timbers, which gave ample opportunity for a little horseplay with which we entertained Kenney from time to time.

Clyde Coulter, the night jailer, was the chief conspirator in that. We would drift into the Casino along about 1 or 2 o'clock in the morning and take one of the boxes with a heavy timber underneath it. When we could get in without Kenney seeing us we were pleased, for there would be more of a surprise when the blowoff came. If he saw us, there was sure to be an argument.

"My heavens, boys," he would exclaim, "lay off the shooting, please. There are some tenderfeet here and they won't understand that it is only sport and that they are in no danger, and there'll be the devil to pay."

Whereupon we would promise, on all that was good and holy, that shooting was farthest from our minds, and be shown to one of the boxes with bullet holes in the floor. It depended on circumstances how soon the blowoff came. If there was a big house, and every indication that the crowd would stay until all hours, or if we had good company, it might be three or four hours, but if it was just an ordinary night and not a particularly good show, it might come in half that time. Anyway, sooner or later, Clyde would start a row with a waiter over something or nothing, out would come his trusty six-shooter and bang-bang-bang it would roar, the bullets going into the heavy framework close to the waiter's feet. At the same time Clyde and I would yell at the tops of our voices, and the girls who were with us would scream, furnishing an excellent imitation of a scrap.

The effect was electrical. There would always be some regulars in the house, who would look around with somewhat bored, if amused, expressions. But there would also be some tenderfeet who took it on the run at the first shot and increased their speed at the following discharges. If they were upstairs, they dropped their girls and rushed out of the boxes and downstairs as though Satan were after them. There they met people from the main floor who were in a hurry to get away from there, and the exit was always jammed with tenderfeet trying to fight their way out.

If the girl who was singing on the stage was an old-timer, and if she happened to see us come in, she would keep right on singing "My Mother was a Lady," or whatever her ditty chanced to be, as though shooting out the lights was a part of the program. But if she was a newcomer she would scream and run off the stage, and Jackie Schiller would lead his orchestra into a popular march.

Kenney and the house employees tried to pacify the panic-stricken tenderfeet, but it seldom did any good, at first. They had heard about Butte and its ways and were not at all ambitious to be called as witnesses in a shooting scrape. It was not until they looked around and saw the show going on as usual, with perhaps half of the crowd in their seats and smiling at the uproar that they took courage and some of them went back, while the others went on their way. At that, it probably was an hour or more before things were going smoothly again.

Then ensued the usual heart-to-heart talk with Kenney. Of course he could not go too far without drawing a roast in the Standard or having the cops camping on his trail. But he never failed to go just as far as he dared, which was far enough to accuse Coulter and me of being bandits and burglars and having no respect for the law or for our word. That continued until it palled on us, and on the crowd, by which time we probably had beaten Kenney out of several thousand dollars. But when he cooled off, he took it smilingly as part of the game of Butte.

The three big gambling houses were on Main Street, between Park and Broadway. There was the Combination, which was the largest of the three, run by Morehouse and Albertson, next to Clark's bank, which was on the corner of Main and Broadway. They used to tell tenderfeet that in digging the foundation they took out enough silver ore to pay for the building, which was only partly true. It was a wide and deep hall, with a long bar on each side of the entrance.

There were six or seven faro tables down the wall on either side and an equal number, back to back, in the middle of the room. Each table had its dealer and lookout. There were tables for stud poker in the rear. Upstairs there was another bar and seven or eight more tables, which number could be increased when necessary. Next to the Combination was Joseph (Spot) Satterlee's, which was as big as the Combination but restricted to one floor, and farther down, next to Jacobs' clothing store, which was on the corner of Park Street, was the M&M, run by Sam Martin and William Mosby, which was somewhat smaller.

Spot and I became very good friends after a meeting that promised a shooting. I had not been in a camp a great while before I took a rap at Satterlee's game in a story, on the word of a gambler. When I reached the office the next day, I found word that Spot wanted to see me. If I had been in the camp a little longer I would have understood that this meant trouble but, in all the blissful ignorance of a tenderfoot, I went right down to Spot's. When I went in I noticed that the bartenders and other employees of the place looked at me intently, and it dawned on me later on that they were taking their last look at me alive, as they thought. I inquired for Spot and was told that he was back at the stud games. So I walked back there and found him watching a game for high stakes. Waiting until the hand was finished, I said:

"Spot, I understand you want to see me."

Spot was facing the table, with both hands in his hip pockets. He whirled around, and I noticed that his right hand gripped his gun, though it made no impression on me at the time. He looked me up and down for a full minute, which seemed much longer at the time. Then he said, with much feeling:

"Well, I'll be good and damned! Yes, I want to see you. Come and have a drink."

And he took my arm and we walked to the bar that was on our side of the house. Then he asked me who had given me the story I ran that morning. I told him, of course, for it had

Hell With the Lid Off

not been given to me in confidence—and it was impressed upon me that the man was never seen in the camp again.

"Hell, that dirty sonnykabick is a dirty Welsher and no good at all," said Spot. He explained how the play came up, and I put the thing right the next morning. Later on, Spot became one of the best friends I had in the camp. But he was a killer, and I came to understand that his invitation to call on him was really an invitation to be slain.

Square gamblers took violent umbrage at any aspersions on the honesty of their games. Any man, drunk, sober or a tenderfoot, was safe in any of the three big gambling houses. If he did not see that he had won, the dealer or the lookout would call his attention to it, and it was the same if he lost. If he was too drunk to watch the cards, he was not allowed to play, under any conditions. Faro, which is the fairest of all gambling games and with the smallest percentage going to the house, and stud poker, were licensed, and were the only games that were permitted, though many of the saloons had back rooms in which solo and poker were played by privileged clients. The gambling houses were packed every afternoon and night, and especially on Sundays and holidays.

"Boston Charley" Marion's dump, at the corner of Main and Galena Streets, like many of the smaller places, was of the other type. Craps were shot there, by whites and Negroes, and a two-card box was the ordinary thing. It was looked over by tourists as a curiosity and patronized by the offscourings of the camp.

There was a deviation from the established principles of gambling only once, and then for only a few hours, in the seven years that I was in Butte. That was under the reform administration of Mayor William Thompson when E.J. Tebo was city marshal and S.J. Waters was chief of police. A supposedly shrewd gambler from the East named Bradford Orlopp was responsible for it.

Orlopp looked the ground over with great care, finally taking a room in the lodging house in which I lived, to be near me, as it turned out. He tried to bribe both Tebo and

Waters, but they refused to touch his money. He assayed other methods, which likewise failed, and he came to me with his proposition. I laughed at him.

"This is a wise town," I told him. "If you try to run roulette and chuck-a-luck games here, you will be shot or chased out of town."

He insisted, however, that they would take the money if I handled it. He offered Tebo and Waters $500 a month, in advance, to be divided as they saw fit, and I was to have $250 a month for handling the funds. But I stopped that instantly.

"Maybe I value my life too high," I said, "but I am so sure that I would be shot if it was even suspected that any of the money stuck to my fingers. That, quite apart from the morals of the case, I won't touch it."

However, he was so positive that Tebo and Waters would accept the bribe that I told them of my talk and Orlopp's offer. Greatly to my surprise, they accepted it, with the understanding that I say nothing about it—a promise from which I consider that I am now released. Accordingly, Orlopp gave me $500 one afternoon, which I duly passed on to Tebo and Waters.

The games were to be started the next morning in a saloon just above the M&M gambling house, the rear entrance to which was almost under my window. I was awakened long before noon by a commotion in the joint. There was much loud taking and I heard the roulette game going and the chuck-a-luck wheel spinning. Then it grew more quiet and I went to sleep again. When it got around 1 o'clock the games were suspended, and they did not open again. The recognized gamblers complained to Tebo and he had gone to the saloon in which the barred games were being played. He sent word that he was coming, however, and the games were all put away when he got there. He said he could see nothing, but the odor was so strong that he saw he could not deliver the goods—which I had assured him he would find impossible—in the face of outraged public opinion.

But the money was not returned. I blamed Tebo much more than I did Waters in that transaction, for he dragged Waters into it, but I never had much use for Tebo after that, nor for "reform" administrations.

CHAPTER 9

JAIL GAMES

Tricking the chief of police

Night jailer Frank Anderson was as big as a horse and twice as strong and lightning fast with a gun

Another thing I wanted to know, after having seen a number of men shot and shot at, was what my own reaction would be to fretful and serious-minded gunfire. Never having served as a target for anyone who was ambitious to make more work for the coroner, though frequently threatened, I was naturally curious as to how I would stand the test.

That question was surprisingly answered, in a manner that was satisfactory to me and furnished quite a mess of fun to the good people who were in the conspiracy against me—which included, as nearly as I could estimate, about half the entire population of Butte. It all grew out of the passion for practical joking that possessed us, meaning thereby Sterling J. Waters, chief of police and known to his friends as "Cap," Clyde Coulter, the night jailer, and myself. It started, innocently enough, in some playful pranks and just grew of its own accord, in fertile soil.

The concentrated foolishness had its origin, so far as its outward manifestation was concerned, in the Western card game of solo, or sluff, which, of course, everyone in the camp knew and to which we were all devoted. Sluff is played by three or four men—if by four, the dealer stays out and pays and is paid according to table rules. Thirty-six cards are used, everything from the seven-spot up, of which all are dealt to each player and three go, face downward, into the "widow." When a man frogs, he skins his hand to the widow, which is exposed or not, according to table rules; but in a solo it is never shown to anyone. There are 30 in each suit—the ace counting eleven, the 10-spot ten, king four, queen three and jack two—and sixty is the dividing line. In the case of a frog, hearts are always trump and payment is even; in a diamond, spade or club solo it is two for one, and in a heart solo, which is the top, it is three for one.

The widow lends an air of mystery to the game, which is altogether fascinating. Two are always playing against the one who is playing the hand, and this was, indirectly, the cause of all of my trouble. When one of them takes a trick, or plays the high card, if his partner does not have to follow suit, he "sluffs" his counting cards, which explains the colloquialism in the name. In this way lone tens are gotten rid of, and then the ace of the suit will be found in the widow, sometimes, when the hand has been played out.

We began playing sluff in the jail office late at night on comparatively quiet evenings. The attraction of the game was so strong that officers, when they brought in prisoners, would stand around and watch us. Sometimes there would be three or four around us, giving advice and offering suggestions when a hand was finished, and the thing grew to be something of a scandal. The officers knew that if they dropped into the office at any time after midnight they were reasonably sure to find a sluff game in full-tilt, and there were many visitors on slight pretexts. The result was that the heart of the city was often left with diminished protection, and it was not a great while until Mayor Bill Thompson felt called upon to put a stop to the practice. That made it necessary for me to get an order permitting us to play solo, and the good mayor finally issued the following permit:

SPECIAL PROCLAMATION

Permission is hereby granted to S.J. Waters, Chief of Police, and Clyde C. Coulter and Frank Anderson, jailers, to play solo, or sluff, in the office of the city jail after 12 o'clock, midnight, with Horace Smith, when it does not interfere with police duties; and there must be no gathering of policemen to observe the progress of the games.

WILLIAM THOMPSON, Mayor

We had this neatly framed and hung in the jail office, and I then had control of the situation. Being deprived of our usual audience, except the reporter for the Miner, made it necessary to entertain him. We began this by threatening gunplay, and right there the successive changes in the Miner's police reporters began. One of us would apparently catch another in some funny business with the cards, and immediately there would be an explosion.

"Hey there, Cap, that's enough of that. I saw you, and if there is any more of it I will do some shooting," Coulter would exclaim, pulling his gun and laying it on the table beside him.

"Copping an ace from the played cards," Coulter would explain—though nothing of the kind had happened, of course.

"If there's any shooting, I had better be prepared," I would say, at the same time pulling my gun and placing it close at hand.

"I did nothing of the kind," the Captain would protest, apparently enraged by the imputation of crookedness. "And if you start any shooting, I'll finish it!" And out would come his gun. Frequently guns were waved around quite promiscuously—with fingers always behind the trigger, but that was not noticed. It was all very dangerous and foolish, of course, but it was done for the benefit of the Miner reporter, who invariably had business somewhere else when the game became exciting.

Coulter then conceived the notion of making it stronger by fooling with his six-shooter. We would find him, with the gun in his hands and apparently making a study of the mechanism, at the same time keeping it pointed, most of the time, in the direction of the Miner reporter, who sat on a chair or a bench on the opposite side of the office.

"What's the matter with your gun, Clyde?" Waters or I would ask, at the same time being careful to get out of range.

"Damned thing won't go off and I'm trying to find out what the trouble is."

"Is it loaded?"

"Of course it's loaded," Coulter would say, holding up the pistol so that the ends of the cartridges could be seen. "What would I be doing with an empty gun? And I can't break it to get the loads out."

"Well be careful with it, for heaven's sake," I would say. "There are killings enough around here without one for which there is no excuse."

"I am careful. Here, you take it and see if you can find out what is wrong with it," he would say, offering the weapon to Waters or me. Always the invitation was declined, and he would go ahead with his tinkering.

Pretty soon there would be a bang—and the Miner would need a new police reporter, for no man would remain on a job which was surrounded with so much danger. The cartridge that exploded was a blank, which Coulter had made by extracting the bullet and substituting a wad of blotting paper; there were no blank cartridges in Butte in those days.

That blank cartridge was my undoing. In a burst of confidence, I told Coulter we would scare Waters out of a year's growth some night by picking a fight with him and turning them loose on him. Clyde fell in with the idea with both feet. Then, in the multiplicity of Butte's activities, I forgot about it, temporarily—but Coulter didn't.

One midnight Waters came into the office in an ugly mood, apparently. He seemed to have been drinking and started quarreling with Coulter and me as soon as he opened the door. We looked at him and then at each other.

"The Missourian's drunk," I commented.

Hell With the Lid Off

"Plenty," said Coulter. "But we'll teach him some manners. Let's cob him. You get the cob and I'll hold him."

The cob—a rubber hose attached to a handle with which jailers maintained order, of a sort, in the jail—was in the engine room. I rushed out for it while Clyde threw his arms around Waters. Just as I got hold of it there was a shot in the office and Coulter began yelling at the top of his voice. He came tearing out, screaming: "He shot me, he shot me," and, with his hand on his thigh, started climbing on top of the boiler. He played his part to perfection and made as much noise as a bunch of Indians on the rampage.

Instinctively, I rushed for the office. Waters stood in the door with his gun pointed at me. It was not his regular gun, which should have made me suspicious. Instead, it was a seven-shot device held in the palm of the hand, with the barrel protruding between the fingers, and fired by squeezing. It shoots .32 cartridges, as I knew from having seen them, and they are fairly deadly. He fired at my chest, but I dodged and seized him by the shoulders and threw him clear across the outer office. I thought later that was something of a feat, as he weighed over two hundred pounds, more than me, though he was not as tall. I threw him so far, in fact, that I could not get at him quickly, so I slipped in the office and closed the door. By that time, he was prepared to fire again.

With the slamming of the door I became perfectly cool, and I wanted nothing in the world so much as the blood of Waters. That became an obsession with me, so that I could think of nothing else. Coulter, meanwhile, was keeping up a persistent howling in the comfort of the boiler on which he remained perched. The thick oak door, I figured, would fend off any bullets, and Waters must have had the same idea, for he confined his efforts to shooting through the keyhole. One of the wads struck me in the fleshy part of the leg, and I shook my trousers to see the flow of blood. The fact that none came went unnoticed, for my mind was filled with getting even.

Waters had shot Coulter, how badly I did not know, and was trying his best to shoot me, and the only thing to do was to put him out of commission. But what to do it with was the question. Coulter's coonskin overcoat and his undercoat were hanging on the inside of the door, and I shook them thoroughly in search of a gun. As a matter of fact, a two-shot derringer of .45 caliber was in the outside pocket of the undercoat, but luckily it was so light that I overlooked it— that was the one mistake the conspirators made in not hiding all weapons that I might get my hands on. I could not reach the desk, in which ordinarily there were two or three guns—but which had none at all that night—and the only offensive and defensive weapons in sight were two Indian clubs in a far corner.

So I concluded that the only thing I could do was to wait until Waters' gun was empty and then rush across to our office and get my own six-shooter. It struck me as strange that the bullets, which were coming through the keyhole, did not do some damage to the wall, but I was too much occupied with how I would put a bullet into Waters to give the matter serious thought. After six shots had been fired, I left the door unguarded for half a second while I gained possession of the clubs. Then throwing the door open, I started for Waters with the clubs raised—to be met by the seventh shot. I twisted around as the shot was fired and congratulated myself on my escape.

I ducked into the office again to think things over, and the time it took me to remember that the gun Waters was using had seven chambers instead of six gave him almost time enough to reload. Throwing the door open again I rushed out to see Waters, on the far side of the outer office, just completing his reloading. Knowing that I could not reach him before he was ready for business, I hurled both clubs at him and tore out of the office and up the steps and across the street. He fired once just as I reached the outer door, but apparently missed. He ran to the head of the steps and fired several more shots as I went up the alley, but they did not worry me at all, for I knew I could outrun the bullet.

Hell With the Lid Off

As I ran across Broadway I noticed a crowd of unusual size in front of Lange's saloon, and similar crowds in front of the Butte hotel and the California Brewery, but paid no attention to them. It turned out later that they knew I would be along shortly, and that I would be in a hurry. The game was well staged, right enough, and I seemed to be about the only man in town who was not in the know.

Tearing into the office, I went to my desk and looked in the drawer where my gun was usually kept. But it was not there, nor in any other part of the desk. If my mind had not been entirely filled with getting even with Waters, this would have made me smell a rat. I frisked all of the other desks in the office, but not a gun was to be found. Bob Curran, our operator, was the only other man in the office, but he walked nonchalantly back and forth and was apparently quite uninterested in my search. Finally it occurred to me that there was a little Flobert rifle available, of .22 caliber, with which we used to shoot mice, and while that did not seem a very efficient weapon with which to combat a .32 caliber pistol, I figured that if I could get Waters in the eye it would do the business. So I loaded the rifle with all of the cartridges it would hold, slipped it under my overcoat and started back to the jail. Curran innocently asked where I was going with the gun. I told him over to the city hall to shoot some rats—or one rat. Then he looked at me and laughed.

"For Heaven's sake, aren't you on yet?" he asked.

Then a great light dawned over Israel—and I proceeded to buy the necessary drinks, though, strangely enough, Waters and Coulter insisted that they should provide the liquid refreshments.

Going home that morning, Fred Parlin—the policeman on the beat where I lived—met me on the street.

"Say," he said, "you want to watch yourself tonight. Waters and Coulter are figuring on giving you the works, somehow. I heard them talking about it, but that was all I heard."

"Not tonight, Fred; it was last night," I told him.

PRANKS WITH COULTER AND THE CHIEF

However well I had stood the test, that was an insult that demanded some retribution, and it was not a great while in coming. This time Coulter was my partner. Waters was very much taken, at the time, with a woman who lived down near Meaderville, in the extreme eastern end of the camp. He had kept his attachment for her very much under the rose and supposed that Coulter and I were entirely innocent of it, which we would have been had not the policeman on the beat whispered it to me. So I made her a party to the plot. In certain devious ways it was arranged that the next time Waters called he was to be persuaded to leave all of his clothes in the outer room, and she was to leave the front door unlocked. I was to be advised of the date by the friendly policeman, who must be credited with alert supervision over that particular house as long as was necessary.

In due course, perhaps a month later, I was advised by the smart patrolman that Cap was in the house and the trap was set, according to the program. I hustled down there and quietly slipped in the front door, and took every stitch of clothes the Captain had, including his shoes, and took them to the city jail office, where we removed a handsome, diamond-studded badge which had been given him by some of his devoted admirers. First we went to Whatley's restaurant, which was best in camp, with two others and quietly partook of an elaborate supper, with wine and all the trimmings. We left the diamond badge as security, with the explanation that Waters would call and settle the bill and redeem the badge. That was all right with Whatley, who suspected there was a hen on.

Then we set out to complete the arrangements. Waters roomed in a building at Arizona and Park Streets which was populated largely by theatrical and sporting people, whose menfolk did not get home until five or six in the morning. After tipping them off as to what was about to happen, and enlisting their warm support, we adjourned to the eastern suburbs, hard by the cottage in which the gay Captain was

Hell With the Lid Off

enjoying himself. We first cut loose with our six-shooters, only a short distance away from the house, and just out of sight of it, mixed with a lot of yelling and groaning. In the dead of night, in one of the most quiet parts of town, it sounded as though somebody was murdering his whole family.

At the first shot Waters made a hurried scamper for his clothes. No clothes at all—only a note on the chair explaining the unimportance of shooting off blank cartridges. That gave him something to think about while he was waiting.

It would never do for the chief of police to expose himself in nothing but his underwear, for it was the dead of winter for one thing. And for another, Waters was part of a reform administration that frowned on such escapades. So there was nothing for him to do but possess his soul in patience while he waited for the officer on the beat to come around. And he was a long while coming, for he explained that he was trying to locate the promiscuous fusillade and the cause of it.

"Never mind about that," said the Captain. "Get me a hack, and keep your mouth shut."

Getting a carriage at that hour of the morning in a residential part of the camp was something of a chore, but one finally was obtained. If it took longer than was necessary it could not be proved and, wrapped only in a blanket, Cap climbed into it from the back door.

Arriving at his rooming house he slipped out, when no one appeared to be in sight, and crept up the stairs. On the stairway a man he did not know, and whose face could not be made out in the semi-darkness handed him his clothes, in which were his keys, and his money, which we did not touch. At the head of the stairs was a long hallway, which was lighted by only one weak bulb, and Waters' room was at the extreme end. Cap paused at the head of the stairs long enough to fish his keys out of the pocket of his trousers and then started down the hall.

But before he had taken two steps I snatched off the blanket that protected him from the wintry blasts, Coulter threw a switch that lighted every bulb in the hall, and we both let out a roar: "Run you Missouri sonnykabick, run." Every door in the hall flew open to see the chief of police running down the passageway, attired only in his underclothes.

The curtain may as well be drawn over the later events that night. But that broke Waters of the habit of shooting at people with blanks just to see them run, and we got along like six in a bed after that.

As evidence of the wonderful camaraderie that existed among us, despite the pranks some two of us were forever playing on the third member of the triumvirate, it was not a great while after this that I heard of a shell game being worked in Conner & Doyle's Collar and Elbow saloon, a drunk and disorderly dump among a score of equally disgraceful resorts on the south side of east Park Street. I mentioned it to Waters, thinking he had heard of it too, but it was news to him.

"Let's go see," said Cap, leading the way. As has been stated, none of the police wore anything that looked like a uniform. And there was nothing about Waters to suggest that he was in any way different from the crowd. The only mark of authority he carried was his diamond-studded badge—which he had retrieved from Joe Whatley the night after our big supper—and which was pinned to his vest. With his undercoat buttoned up he looked like a shift-boss. And it was easy for him to assume a half-intoxicated condition, but his mind was working full tilt all of the time. He had a very disarming way with him, and in such a situation it was comparatively simple for him to be sized up as a sucker.

We sauntered into the Collar and Elbow and there, at the back of the saloon, was a gathering around a man who was calling on the crowd to watch his hands closely, to see under which shell he placed the pea. The men seemed unable to do so with any regularity judging by the growing size of his bankroll. He had his back to a window, which was one story above the ground, on account of the side hill upon which the camp stood. It was Sunday night, when you had to walk in the street if you wanted to make time, and the gambler probably thought he could make a stake before the police got wise. Furthermore, from the nature of the place, he expected to be tipped off when the cops appeared. But Cap pulled his cap down over his eyes and turned his overcoat collar up and slouched into the place, and he was overlooked in the crowd.

Waters waited the game for a few moments, waving around as if he had a good half load aboard, and then put down a $5 gold piece—and won. He displayed a pocket full of money, and the dealer evidently thought that here was a sure-enough sucker. He paid the bet, and Waters let it all ride. He won again, and the process was repeated. Then, on the third play, he lost. The dealer was just raking in the money when Cap interfered.

"I'll take that, and you too," he said, as he threw open his coat and pushed all of the money on the table into his cap, which I held for him. The dealer, the instant he saw the chief's badge, backed into the window, sat down in it and rolled out, heels overhead, into two feet of snow and got up running, though there was no pursuit. Waters and I went outside where we divided the money, which amounted to over $600.

"We'll just play what we fined him," explained Waters, "only we won't enter it on the blotter. It's too bad that Coulter is on the day shift, but that gives more for us. What do you say?"

I said all right, for that was money I had no qualms about taking, some of it having come from miners who had bad eyesight, and who otherwise would have spent it for liquor.

Frank Anderson, years later a member of an international rifle team, was then the night jailer and a source of constant worry to us. He was as big as a horse, and twice as strong and lightning fast with a gun. His only defect was a leg that had been broken in a mine at the knee and so badly set that it bowed greatly, though not enough to interfere in any degree with his agility. Dozens of times I have seen him, when he had an unruly mob of prisoners in the jail, go in alone and lock the grated door behind him, so that if they got him right they could have murdered him a dozen times before we could get to him by breaking down the door. But they never got him right, nor anywhere in that vicinity.

He would walk right in among the prisoners, but was always careful not to leave a space at his back for a surprise attack. His gun was in its holster at his belt, but his hands were far from it. He would ask what the trouble was about and who was responsible for it. If they told him, the disturbers were locked up in a separate cell. If they didn't he would nag at them until finally, a man more daring than the rest, and sometimes two or three of them, would reach for his gun.

Then Frank sprang into action: His hand went to the weapon so fast that the eye could not follow it. It came out as quickly and was used as a club, so fast and furiously that a mob of a dozen or more would be knocked this way in two or three seconds. The men who were not knocked down and out threw themselves on the floor and begged for mercy. If any of the ringleaders resorted to these tactics Frank would put his gun away, drag them to their feet with his left hand and then hit them in the face, just once. That was generally enough to render them unconscious. Then, with quiet restored for the night, Frank would casually examine the wounded to see whether any of them needed medical attention—which they frequently did—and then open the door and walk out, perfectly unaffected by the disturbance.

Anderson was a playful person, too, but not of the devil-may-care type that was Coulter. And he sure was handy with his hardware. But, quick as he was with a gun, he was just as clever with a rifle. So I was not surprised to read, years later, that he was good enough to make an international team and be sent abroad.

The people of Butte were quite particular, though careless themselves, as to the manner in which the pocket weapons that most of the men carried were described. They were popularly known as guns, though six-shooter was occasionally used. Some of the old Vigilantes, quaintly enough, referred to them as pistols and revolvers. But at least nine times out of ten, a pocket weapon of .42, .44 or .45 caliber was spoken of as a gun; anything smaller was recognized as only a plaything or a toy. If a man who did not have the indistinguishable mark of the West on him spoke of a pocket gun as a revolver, he was at once set down as a tenderfoot who was trying to get away with a bluff.

Only rarely—not more than a dozen times at the most—did I hear the term "two-gun man," and then only in derision to indicate someone who posed as bad but was not really dangerous. No one in Butte needed two guns anyway; if he could not do damage enough with one, he needed the militia. And not in a single instance did I hear the expression "six-gun," which is the sure and certain mark of the tenderfoot, though it has come into common use today, thanks to the films, which produce all sorts of quick and imaginary artists who shoot from the hip with deadly accuracy—in the movies! I knew many men who were expert shots, at live targets and otherwise, but I never knew one, or heard of one, who made any pretense of shooting from the hip. That is one thing that just can't be done with any degree of accuracy at all.

Bob Davis—who writes with the tip of a rainbow dipped in ink distilled from the Aurora Borealis—has fallen into the ways of his Eastern confreres, for he used "six-gun" at least twice in his stories. At his second offense I wrote him an abusive letter, of the kind that one friend writes to another. I told him, among other things, that if he ever heard "six-gun" used in the West it must have been from sheepherders who were barred from contact with real men, and apparently they had been his only contacts.

Bob wrote back a long and equally abusive letter, which was typewritten, but right across the face of it he had inscribed, in red ink: "You're right, at that!"

Which shows that Davis is basically honest. But if he had filled the hand with Waters and Coulter, he never would have used that tenderfoot term.

The Anaconda

ANACONDA, MONTANA. WEDN

BUTTE'S NIGHT OF HORROR

Scores of People Blown Into Atoms By M terious Explosions.

HEROIC FIREMEN MEET THEIR DO

The Darkest and Saddest Page In the History of This Comm wealth—While Surrounding a Fire Near the Montana C tral Depot Many People Were Mowed Down Withou Second's Warning—More Than Forty Dead Bodies covered—Scenes Never Before Equalled In This Part of World for Heartrending Affliction—Cruel Deeds of Deat It Came Like the Crack of Doom----Hundreds of Sadde Hearts----Hospitals Filled With Wounded and Dying---- Streets Crowded With Heartbroken Survivors.

CHAPTER 10

ON THE SCENE OF BUTTE'S WORST DISASTER

"The ground was covered with arms, legs and the bloody remains of the victims of the explosions - Everybody's killed"

It was by the merest accident—if important accidents actually happen in real life—that I escaped being mixed up in the greatest disaster Butte ever knew. And if I had been mixed up in it, this story never would have been written. The reader, therefore, will be able to judge as to whether it really was an accident, in fact. Me, I don't think that it was, but rather one of those interesting innovations of fate, by whatever name you choose to call It, that I have encountered several times in the course of a fairly active life.

It happened about 9 o'clock in the evening of January 15, 1895. A fire alarm came in from the box near the Montana Central depot. I was writing a story at the time but ran to the door to see the firemen come out, as the central station was directly opposite our office and the members of the department were all my friends. I was in the habit of riding to fires with them, and as the hose wagon swung around in front of the shop the boys on the back end moved closer together to make a place for me and two of them reached out their hands to catch me. I started to run for it—but was called back by Bob Curran, our operator, who begged me "for Heaven's sake come back and finish that story."

So I went back. It was not an important yarn I was writing. But I knew that Bob was sending it as I wrote, and to run off with it unfinished would leave both ends of the wire up in the air. I completed the tale and was at the telephone to inquire about the fire.

"Where's the blaze?" I asked the clerk in the Montana Central freight station.

"No fire down here," he replied.

"An alarm just came in from your box."

"Wait a minute and I'll go out and see." And the interruption saved his life, for while he was outside, between lines of freight cars, the first explosion let go and flattened the freight house like a pancake. Had he been inside he would certainly have been killed under the mass of debris instead of simply shaken up a bit.

George Pascoe, an alderman, came in from the city hall and asked where the fire was. I was at the telephone, waiting, and I told him I was just finding out. Then the first explosion came with a bright flash that lit up all of the region in the vicinity.

"There's our fire, and it looks as though it had struck an oil tank," I said.

The words were hardly out of my mouth when the concussion came along—and the big window of the Northern Pacific office, on the other side of the building from ours, went in with a crash. Strange to say, I did not at first connect the rush of wind with the fire. Feeling was then pretty high between the Catholics and the American Protective Association, and my first impression was that one side or the other had planted a bomb under our building and that it would be toppling around our heads in about one and a half seconds.

I don't know how I did it, for Pascoe was outside of the railing and much closer to the door, while I had to open a grilled door and take some very rapid steps. But I beat him outside and raced across the street. I started for the city hall but remembered that it was made of brick and might come tumbling down too. So I ran straight ahead to the California Brewery, which was a big frame building, backed up against it and looked at our building, It was undamaged, except for one broken window. But just then bundles of rakes and shovels, which were thrown as far north as Walkerville, two miles away, came falling down out of the sky, and there was the noise of crinkling glass on all sides.

I connected the explosion with the fire, ran back to the office, got my overcoat and jumped in a hack and told the driver to break all records in getting to the fire. We were halfway there when the police stopped us, as they were turning everybody back, but they waved him ahead when they saw who was in the hack. He was just starting when the second explosion went off. Remembering the broken windows, I presumed the front windows of the hack would be blown in, with great force. With a proper regard for my eyes, I jumped out and ran across the street, taking refuge between two frame residences. For two or three minutes I was kept busy dodging falling missiles and watching a bundle of shovels that landed on the electric light wires just over head.

When the storm of debris subsided, the hack was nowhere in sight. So I walked the rest of the way. But for the police, I had the street to myself, just a short distance above the fire, which I could see plainly. Then a third explosion let go.

The sidewalk there was three or four feet above grade and I ducked under it, while pieces of iron and bricks rattled down. The third explosion, however, was much less violent than the first two and did little damage. I climbed out to pick my way diagonally across a large vacant lot, with the blazing ruins of some warehouses in the far corner, absolutely deserted. The ground was covered with arms, legs and the bloody remains of the victims of the explosions.

Watching my step to see that I did not walk on any of the fragments that had been men a few minutes before, or fall into a pool of blood, I was halfway across the lot when I met Red Gray, a Montana Central switching crew conductor.

"Where are you going?" he asked.

To the fire, I told him.

"They tell me the firemen are all killed. Everybody's killed. You'd better stay away," he replied.

"All the more reason why I should be there. I'm going to see if I can find someone who is still alive." I told the conductor.

"Wait a minute. Do you see that car?" He pointed to a freight car that was just beginning to burn at the roof.

"Well, that car is full of dynamite, too; the same stuff that killed all of these people," he said, swinging his arms around.

"How do you know?"

"Because I switched it in there myself this afternoon."

"Thank you," I said, and turned right around and headed the other way, walking as fast as I could. As a matter of fact, the car to which Red pointed was empty; something like his head, at the time. He was watching the fire from where he was working, which was a safe distance; then came the first explosion, and there were no people left standing. The shock proved too much for him. It was several days before he regained his senses.

I hurried to the office and told Wally of the scene, then went on the rounds of the undertakers and hospitals. There were only two undertakers but there were several large hospitals. I had the run of all of them and knew all of the doctors.

What had happened was that a fire, which ordinarily would have been easily handled, had started in one of three warehouses that adjoined each other on a siding of the Montana Central, not far from the depot. Dynamite composition from the Giant Powder Company was stored in the warehouses, in flagrant violation of the law. Railroad metal fishplates were stacked in front of dynamite in metal rabble-heads, six inches long and three inches wide, used to pull the slag off the furnaces. The stacks of fishplates kept people from shooting into the dynamite and exploding it. But, because it was against the law, there were no signs posted and no one connected with the warehouses had sense enough to warn the firemen of the danger.

The fishplates were piled deep and high, and well served the purpose for which they were intended. But they proved to be deadly missiles, responsible for many deaths. The rabble-heads shot out like smooth stones and cut off arms and legs, or heads, or went right through a man at a considerable distance from the fire. These objects accounted for the ghastly condition in the field which I attempted to cross on my way to the fire. In the undertaking parlors I saw bodies that were decapitated by flying rabble-heads and others the rabble-heads or fishplates had gone through, scattering entrails.

The firemen, naturally, were right on top of the fire, and they were literally blown to pieces. Angus Cameron, the chief, had a very heavy moustache. They found half of it, which was easily recognized. Pieces of what was supposed to be Jack Sloan, the assistant chief, were buried together in one baby's coffin.

Dave Magee, the driver of the hose wagon, was the only fireman who escaped. He ran two lines of hose to the fire and then drove back a short distance and was covering his horses with a blanket raised between himself and the fire when the first explosion let go. The horse nearest to it was blown to pieces; the second, too, was killed, landing on Dave and breaking his leg. He reached home, had his leg set and sent word to me that if I would come down, he would tell me all he knew about the fire. That was one of the finest exhibitions of friendship I encountered, in that home of strong friends.

Fortunately the fire occurred in the winter when the powder was frozen and did not explode until it had been thawed out by the blaze. Only a very small part of it let go, the first explosion scattering the fire to the second, and the second to the third. If it had been summer time, all of the powder would have exploded at once and Butte would have been wiped off the map, with frightful loss of life. Practically the entire loss of life resulted from the first explosion, due to the thickness of the protection against bullets, which made it impossible for more of the dynamite to thaw out before the heat became great enough to set it off.

Hell With the Lid Off

Estimates of the percentage of powder that exploded ran all the way from 10 to 25. Ten or 15 percent probably came closer to the fact. With bundles of shovels sent great distances and windows broken all over the camp, one can only imagine what would have happened if all of that dynamite went up at the same time. Lines of freight cars were wrecked and the freight house flattened. But the depot, which was some distance away and protected by strings of cars, was saved. Broken sticks of powder were scattered all over the countryside. Most of this was picked up by the police the next day. But hundreds of pieces were gathered by tourists as souvenirs of the catastrophe.

The next morning I found Donald McLaren, the division superintendent of the Montana Central, who had come down from Havre 300 miles away during the night on a special train, pounding a piece of debris on the counter of the ticket office, which was closed. I saw what he was doing, and before I could move he rather impatiently asked a question.

"What is this stuff, anyway?"

"Nothing but dynamite," I told him.

He'd been just about to give the counter another rap with it. His face went white and he began to shake although he was about six feet tall and weighed all of 225 pounds.

"JESUS CHRIST," he said, as he laid the stick down gently and went out of the office on tip-toe.

Fifty-seven people were killed that night, in a moment, and the Standard had the names of 56, and one unidentified, the next morning.

Editor's note: The Wednesday, Jan. 16 Anaconda Standard story of the disaster ran under the headline BUTTE'S NIGHT OF HORROR. Subheads read: "Scores of people blown into atoms by mysterious explosions" and "heroic firemen meet their doom." The account differs from Smith's when it comes to identifying casualties: "With the fearful list of the dead, the chief horror is that comparatively few have been identified," it reads, noting the mutilated conditions of many victims.

We certainly threw the fear of the hereafter into the Miner that night. We had nearly three pages, written by four men, and the Miner had barely two columns, half a column of which was the head and another half column a partial list of the dead. And this despite the fact that it was the worst disaster Butte had ever known. I think that was the best piece of straight newspaper work I ever did, and I was full of pride the next morning when I heard the newsboys calling: "Miner. Standards all gone." Our edition was reprinted, for the benefit of people to send back East, until the matrices were burned up. There was no semblance of a race between the Standard and the Miner after that. That was the final blow.

Mr. Daly came into the office the next afternoon with a twinkle in his eye.

"That was a damned good paper you boys got out this morning," he said.

Wally allowed that we all felt the same way about it.

"Yes indeed. I'll say it was good. It cost me a dollar."

It developed that the newsboy on the Tuttle building corner always saved a paper for Mr. Daly when he spent the night in Butte. He held onto one that morning, thought he had many calls for it. The Old Man always gave the boy two-bits for the paper, and he offered him two-bits that morning.

"I can't let you have the paper for two-bits this morning, Mr. Daly," said the boy. "I've been offered four-bits for it."

Whereupon the Old Man handed him a dollar, smiling broadly as he said: "It must be a mighty good paper."

"It is. It's got the Miner skinned to death on the explosion last night."

When the Old Man went out he sent in a case of wine and a box of two-bit cigars for each of us.

Scores of people were more or less seriously injured. They were all at a considerable distance from the fire and were struck by the flying missiles. Everyone who was close to the blaze, without some protection, was blown to pieces or instantly killed. There was much talk about prosecution for storing dynamite within city limits, or for two or three miles on all sides of it, was strictly prohibited. But it all ended in talk and delayed legal proceedings.

Thomas A. Riley, who lost a leg in the explosion, paid a visit to Patrick A. Largey, president of the State Savings Bank and an owner of a warehouse that had caught fire and exploded. Riley said he wanted $10,000. Largey asked the man if he was not getting money regularly from company stockholders. The man replied that he was, but it was not enough to compensate him for the loss of a leg, and he wanted more. Largey said he couldn't give it to him, whereupon Riley pulled a gun and shot Largey to death.

After that, others with financial interest in the companies sold out and moved to southern California.

CHAPTER 11

LIVIN' THE LIFE OF A MINING MILLIONAIRE

The copper war gets settled at sea

F. A. Heinze's wife, an actress who had played a vampire, developed a habit of mysteriously disappearing

In the days when Fritz Augustus Heinze was fighting the Standard Oil Company from soda to hock, and with every shot in the locker, he had more friends than any other man I ever knew. The word friends is used in all of its Western applications, meaning men who not only would cheer for him but fight for him—with guns, fists or anything that was handy. Marcus Daly might have had as many friends if he had time to mix more. Heinze mixed because he had the time and because he figured that their friendship might be useful to him later on. In which prognostication it is known of all men that he was right. It seemed that he knew almost every man in Butte by his first name.

He was easily, by all odds and under all conditions, the best bluffer I ever knew. He fought the Standard Oil Company and the Amalgamated Copper Company all over the lot for years, and whipped them emphatically. If they had known how nearly they had him out 20 times they would, somehow, have added a little steam to their punches and put him away for the count. But they didn't know, and the serenity and sublime confidence with which he faced them, when he was the most tightly pinched, was unruffled. He bluffed them to a standstill a dozen times, or more.

Heinze, who was the son of a German Lutheran minister and who graduated from the Columbia School of Mines as a mining engineer, reached Butte in 1889, on the same train with Jimmy Leys, a quiet and canny Scot. Jimmy started a small jewelry store, saved his money and later moved on to New York and became a manufacturer of pink pearls and other things, living next door to William Boyce "Boulder" Thompson, a mining engineer who was born in Montana. Heinze got a job underground, as a mining engineer, for the Boston & Montana Company.

He was working at that, during the day, when I landed in the camp, picking up information that was to be of value to him later on. At night, he frequented all of the saloons, in turn, and made friends with the miners, gathering bits of gossip about veins and dips and angles and spurs, which was carefully catalogued. He saw the need of a smelter to handle custom ores from the many independent mines, organized the Montana Ore Purchasing Co., and built one.

He trapped James A. Murray into signing a lease on one of his mines which had become profitable, under an agreement to pay an enticing royalty on all ore running above 15 per cent—and then mixed native rock with the ore underground so that not a ton exceeding the 15 percent was hoisted as long as the lease ran. That stamped Heinze as a genius—maybe an evil genius—for it was not easy to hook Murray in a business deal, and the camp gloated. Murray took it with a smile, for he had enough money so that the loss of the royalty did not cause him to go hungry, though it chastened his pride to be tricked by a tenderfoot.

Heinze took a lease on the Glengarry, in the flat south of the camp, in which two or three old-timers had searched in vain for copper, and started a drift in a new direction. Within two or three weeks he opened up a big and rich vein. That gave the hard-headed old mining men something to think about, and they concluded that there might be something after all of importance learned at schools specializing in geology.

As his prosperity increased, Heinze took on new airs and became something of a social lion. He was at all times master of himself and the master of men. He had the manner and all of the graces of a gentleman, which set him apart from every other mining man, with the polish of one to the manor born, which made him idolized by the women. Whether attired in evening clothes or mining togs, he was at home in a drawing-room or a saloon. He was quick at repartee and always had an answer ready for any question under the sun. Someone, seeking to flatter him, told him he "looked like a Greek god," which really was not far from the truth, for he certainly was a handsome chap, about 5 feet 11 inches tall and with the figure of an athlete. But that little pleasantry almost ruined Heinze, just the same, for always after that, until he brought misfortune on himself, he was posing in an effort to live up to his reputation. He lived on the top floor of the post office building and his apartment was the scene of royal entertainment.

The Amalgamated Copper Company had just been formed and the copper war was entering its first stage when I left Butte. Judge William Clancy, whose nomination was secured by trickery and whose election was promoted by Heinze, had just taken the bench and was prepared to pass on the most momentous litigation in the world. Every decision he rendered was in favor of Heinze. Sometimes he would take time to render a decision and declare from the bench: "I will take this matter under advisement for one week—when I will decide in favor of Heinze."

The story of the long fight has been told elsewhere, and as I did not see it I do not propose to talk about it. But here are some interesting things connected with it which have never seen the light of day. One has to do with the settlement of the war.

John MacGinnis, one of Heinze's chief lieutenants—the other being Thomas R. Hinds, a royal Irishman—was the man with whom H.H. Rogers made the terms that ended the war. MacGinnis and Hinds, incidentally, were a wonderful team. MacGinnis was a gentleman, quiet and suave, whose mind was always in high gear while his feet were in low—so low that he was almost invariably late in his appointments. But he was such a lovable chap that his excuses never failed to appease the anger of whoever it was that was kept waiting. Hinds was exactly the opposite—nervous and high strung and always ready to tell every man exactly what he thought of him and his ways, though he didn't release the valves if he was in negotiation with him. But he was like MacGinnis in that his word was as good as gold, once it was passed. The pair made a truly great team, and if Heinze had stuck to them, and followed their advice, he would never have come the cropper that he did.

MacGinnis bought Heinze's United Copper Company and made shares available through Hallgarten & Co., a New York investment company. He later became the firm's unofficial copper adviser and saved them much money. Men from the West were active in New York at that time, and, before they became well acquainted with MacGinnis, Hallgarten and other Wall Street men considered it smart to try to stand them on their heads and shake the money out of their pockets. But it may be said they seldom succeeded.

"How is it, John," asked the elder Hallgarten one day, "that we have such bad luck with you Westerners? When we go into a deal to take something from you, we lose in most cases. But when you undertake to get something from us, you almost always win."

"That's easy," replied MacGinnis. "When you go into a deal against us, you have to spend 75 percent of your time watching each other, which leaves you only twenty-five percent of the time to watch us. We don't have to watch each other at all and can spend all of our time watching you."

"I think you're right," said Hallgarten, after a moment's thought. And that ended the assaults of the East on the West.

One day in 1906, McGinnis was sitting in his New York office when he received a message from Henry Huttleston Rogers, the financier who had made his fortune in oil refining. How would you like to go out riding in my yacht some afternoon? the message read. That appealed to MacGinnis and soon after he was at the New York Yacht Club station on the East River at 4 o'clock when a boat came ashore from Roger's floating palace to gather him.

McGinnis was the only guest and he and Rogers indulged in a general conversation about the price of pork, and other things, until dinner time. Rogers referred to Heinze, as he had often before, with the expletives eliminated, as an "impossible pirate" with whom he would not deal under any terms, and said if the copper war was to be settled it was up to the two of them to agree on terms. He did not say, in so many words, that they were whipped and ready to quit, but he did say he thought the fight had lasted long enough. As they went down to dinner Rogers cautioned McGinnis to say nothing at the table that could give cause for gossip.

"Not a word about the copper war," he said. "The butler has been with me 30 years, and has my entire confidence, but this subject is not for him to overhear."

After dinner they went out aft, and, with a sailor pacing the deck amidships, talked until midnight and ended the long fight. Rogers agreed to pay Heinze $12,500,000 in cash, and a block of Amalgamated stock, for all of Heinze's properties in Montana and an agreement on his part to get out of the copper business and stay out. Heinze and John D. Ryan, president of the Amalgamated, came from Montana to thrash out details. But it was the onboard discussions between MacGinnis and Rogers that terminated the long struggle—for the time being.

THE ALLEGED MR. FIXIT

While Judge Clancy's decisions were a foregone conclusion, there was a great deal of curiosity in Butte, as well as in Wall Street, as to how the jury trials to which Heinze was occasionally subjected, were practically always of the same unanimity. It was suspected that some sort of skullduggery was responsible for them, but the Amalgamated lawyers and the public were equally in the dark, for this was one of Heinze's most carefully guarded secrets. Only four men were acquainted with all of the facts and their lips were sealed. But it can do no harm, at this late date, to describe the method.

It was all in the selection of the jury. The officer of the court whose duty it was to draw the panel from names in a box was on Heinze's payroll—and he was very well paid indeed. As he is still alive, we will call him Mr. Fixit.

The names of those who were on the lists of possible jurors were known some time in advance and Mr. Fixit memorized them carefully, so that he would know what to do when it came to putting them in the box. He had a little dab of paste beside the box, and if the man was unfriendly to Heinze, he put the slip in the mucilage and then pressed it down on the bottom.

The names of Heinze's friends, therefore, were free to come out of the box at a slight shake. The result was that the juries were usually made up entirely of Heinze's fellows. In any event, there was certain to be some of his henchmen impaneled, and the worst he could get would be a hung jury.

The Heinze organization had all sorts of code words, but the one that was paramount and imperative was Snohomish. The receipt of a telegram with that word in it meant that the man who got it should drop everything and hasten to the sender. When Heinze was under indictment in New York for violation of the banking law, after he saw the list of the men from whom the jury that tried him was to be drawn, he sent a Snohomish telegram to John MacGinnis, who came as fast as a train could carry him from the Pacific coast. He told

Heinze that he had no business sending him that message. He changed his mind somewhat when he saw the panel from which the jury would be drawn.

It was more than half made up of men who were, or had been, affiliated with the Standard Oil Company or some of its subsidiaries, and were inimical to Heinze. The state was avowedly out to "get" Heinze, and it looked as though the district attorney had been fraternizing with his foes. MacGinnis and Ryan, Amalgamated's president, had been good friends through all of the row. As general purchasing agent for the Anaconda Company, MacGinnis had given Ryan his first order when he came to Butte as a salesman for the Continental Oil Company. So MacGinnis went directly to Ryan and asked him about the Standard Oil-stacked list. Ryan assured him, on his honor, that there was no foundation for his natural suspicions and that he had never seen it and knew nothing about it.

MacGinnis told Heinze that there was nothing to do but send for Mr. Fixit, which he did. Mr. Fixit came on, with his wife, and took an apartment in the same building with the officer of the court who put the names of the panel in the box. They were both of the same religious faith and were very soon getting along swimmingly. Just what happened may not be told, but the jury acquitted Heinze, though Charles W. Morse was sent to jail for a similar offense involving federal banking laws. There was great jubilation when Heinze was turned loose.

When Heinze got his 12 and half million dollars and a big block of stock, he forgot that he owed MacGinnis a good deal more than a million, and Thomas R. Hinds just as much, and left them to fend for themselves. I did not know this until after Heinze's death. MacGinnis, undaunted, proceeded to make another fortune for himself. And Hinds went to Canada in the railroad contracting business,

I saw very little of Heinze when he came East, with his pockets bulging with money, though I was in New York at the time. He had had plenty of friends then. But after he got in trouble, through the collapse of the bank he had bought and after he had been shown the ways of Wall Street by men who were much wiser than he, I went to him and offered to help him in any way I could. The concerns with which I was connected would have cut me off at the pockets if I had accepted a retainer from Heinze, but they could not complain if I gave him my services because we had known each other in Montana. The more I saw of him then the less I liked him, but I stuck for old times' sake. He had a few mining properties left, chiefly in the Coeur d'Alene area, and at the time of this death he was trying to get control of a lot of sugarcane-growing land in Texas.

John MacGinnis and Tom Hinds came to New York some time after Heinze's acquittal to help him celebrate and also to see if he wanted to sell any of his properties. I knew them both well, and they were far from bargain buyers; they had been pals with Heinze too long to take advantage of his misfortunes, even though he had forgotten all about his obligation to them. I said something about their arrival to Heinze.

"Yes," he said, sarcastically, "they're here to see what they can pick up at the forced sale."

"That remark comes with darned bad grace from you," I replied, and he made no response.

TIPPING WITH A KING

I had dinner one night with Heinze and his lawyer and some turn in the conversation made me say: "F.A., you've got too many 'yes men' around you and not enough to say no. You're not right all of the time on all subjects."

"That's right, Mr. Heinze, that's right," agreed the lawyer, heartily, but he would have remained silent if I hadn't opened the pot.

I told him once that I wouldn't put a dollar in a bank he controlled.

"Why not?" he asked, in surprise, "I'm honest."

"I think you're honest," I said, "but I know you're a mining man and a speculator. Now that Marcus Daly is dead, I'd back your hand in a mine, but that is different from backing your hand in a bank."

In 1910, Heinze married Bernice Henderson, an actress (whose roles had included vampire) who looked like a million dollars when she was dressed for the stage, and much less in ordinary attire. Marriage palled her, and she developed a habit of mysteriously disappearing now and then. Once she was gone for days, and all trace of her was lost. Walking into the Waldorf bar one day, I saw Heinze sitting in a corner with a telegram in one hand and a glass in the other. He saw me at the same time and motioned me over to the seat beside him. As I approached, he thrust the telegram in my hand. It was from the superintendent of a sanitarium in Cincinnati, or some other Ohio town, saying that Bernice had just shown up there and for him not to worry, as she would be home in a few days. Heinze seemed covered with gloom and very much depressed.

"What am I supposed to do?" I asked him. "Break down and cry or give three cheers?"

Heinze wagged his head, in the way he had when he was asked a question that was too deep for him.

"You had it right out in Butte," I added. "When your lady love did something you didn't like, you turned her out with a pocketful of money and got a new one. But you reached the momentous decision that you needed a wife. Having come to that conclusion you went to the largest lemon orchard you could find, selected the largest tree, and took the biggest lemon on it. And now you want sympathy. Try someone else, F.A."

Heinze smiled, then, and cheered up considerably. "By golly I think you're right," he said. "Have a drink."

Two or three weeks later Heinze told his friend, Carlos Warfield, with fine scorn: "That's a fine trust you married men have. Before I was married I thought every married friend I have was perfectly happy. But since I joined the union they tell the truth, and I know damned well that not one of them is happy."

Two years later there was a divorce. There was talk of a reconciliation. And a year later Heinze died, in Saratoga Springs, from a hemorrhage of the stomach caused by cirrhosis of the liver. He was 44.

The strangely tragic thing about it was that of all the thousands of friends he had there was not one who could sincerely say he was sorry. And, take it from me, that is not a good way for a red-blooded man to go, for he is starting on a journey on which he will need the companionship of friendly thoughts, at least.

BOULDER THOMPSON'S UNLIKELY SUCCESS

William Boyce "Boulder" Thompson went the same way. Boulder, so nicknamed from the rocks among which he was raised—though that was not the exact reason—was born in Virginia City, Montana, the son of William Thompson, who would become a mayor of Butte. The elder Thompson was a fine, upstanding little bow-legged man who would tell any man his right name and fight at the drop of the hat. He had two brothers whose names, I think, were James and Edward. James was the treasurer of the Butte football team and he was the only one I knew; the only one, in fact, who was considered worth knowing. Later on he went to Tacoma, where he prospered and died. It was James who said, in New York, when some men were talking of the difficulty they had in seeing Boulder in his office: "It's the same way with me. I never get to him in his office."

Boulder went to school in Virginia City, and I was delighted when I ran across Harry Rogers in New York and found that he was also born in Virginia City and had gone to school with Thompson. He fully verified all I had said, as to Boulder's intelligence, and more, for they had a "dunce stool" in the school, and Harry said Boulder almost wore it out. The family moved to Butte when Boulder was young, and he lived there in comparative idleness, until his father gave him $1,000 and told him to get out and shift for himself.

"I don't know what will happen to Will," the elder Thompson said one day. "He is too lazy to work, and I don't see how he is going to eat if he doesn't do a little work anyway."

Boulder took his $1,000 and headed for Boston. On the train he met an old prospector with what promised to be a copper mine, and he was on his way to Boston to finance it.

"Let's organize a company and sell stock," said Boulder. The stranger agreed, so with Boulder's thousand dollars they formed a company and rented an office and Boulder began sending out letters that he wrote on the typewriter himself. They caught the copper wave on the upswing, and the money began coming in, a trickle at first but gradually increasing until it became a stream. Whatever else may be said of Boulder, he was honest—he couldn't have been less with the father he had—and so was the mining man. The money went into the ground, and before long Thompson sold his interest in the mine for $500,000. After that it was the Nippising silver mine in Canada and, despite his limited intelligence and a wholly unattractive personality, Boulder was on his way to making millions.

H.H. Rogers met Thompson in lower Broadway one day, shortly before Boulder was stricken with a fatal illness. Harry tried to give him the quick pass, for he felt just as I did. I never called on Boulder during all of the years we were in New York together, though friends of both tried more than once to get us together. But on Broadway Thompson flagged him, and they stepped to the edge of the walk.

"Why don't you ever come up to see me, Harry?" inquired Boulder, seemingly much hurt by his friend's lack of interest in getting together.

"Well, I'm uptown, you know, and you're downtown, and every time I get down this way I'm in a hurry, and you're very busy," explained Harry.

"That's not it; you'd come if you wanted to, right enough. None of my old friends come to see me...Well, it probably wouldn't do you much good if you did. There's a fellow at the door with a row of brass buttons on the front of his coat, and you likely wouldn't get past him. If you did, and got to my secretary, she would tell you that I was in conference and couldn't be disturbed, and I probably wouldn't know you had been there at all. It's tough not to see any of your old friends, though, that's what it is."

"I'll come in, some time," said Harry. Then, to make conversation, for Thompson did not seem to want to let him go, he asked about his wife, whom he knew as well as he knew Boulder.

"Not very well. When I got into the big money I had to stay out a good deal at night and she got it into her head that I was running around with other women," Boulder said. "So my home life is not very pleasant, and life at the office is not very pleasant, either. I do wish you would come up to see me, soon and often."

Harry promised, with his fingers crossed, that he would visit. And he got away. Boulder had a stroke in 1924 and died in Yonkers, New York, 1930, at age 61. Like Heinze, many who had known Boulder could not honestly say they grieved his passing. But his new friends, who knew him only in Wall Street, made a great show of their sorrow, real or feigned. For had he left behind a mess of millions.

CHAPTER 12

CLOSE ENCOUNTERS WITH THE BARELY ALIVE

A riot on the Glorious Fourth

**Coroner: "What, if anything, did the deceased say to you after you found him?"
Witness: "He didn't say anything. He was dead"**

Human life was the cheapest thing in Butte for years, and the coroner was just about the busiest man in the county. Robbery was the most serious offense on the docket.

This was illustrated in the late 1890s, by which time the camp was becoming rather offensively civilized in the minds of the surviving old trail-blazers, when two men who had been convicted in the district court came up for sentence before Judge W.O. Speer. The judge was not a bullwhacker, but he had lived in the camp long enough to be classed among the old-timers with whom he fraternized.

One of the prisoners had walked five miles through two inches of snow with a shotgun under his arm and emptied both barrels into the back of a man who was sitting on a log, eating his lunch, literally shooting him in two. The man was unsuspicious of danger and was given no chance for his life, though it was brought out at the trial that the two had been enemies for some time. The prisoner had been convicted of murder in the first degree, with no recommendation from the jury as to his punishment, as was usual in such cases.

In the second case, the defendant was a poor old hobo who, in the dead of winter and with few clothes to cover him, had taken a discarded overcoat that he found hanging in the woodshed of a miner's cabin. To get in, he had forced the lock of the door. The owner of the overcoat testified at the trial that he had no further use for it and that if the tramp had asked for it he would gladly have given it to him. But the unfortunate hobo, knowing nothing of the ways of the West, had neglected to ask for it. So he was convicted of robbery, though petty larceny, at the worst, would have amply covered his case.

The judgments of the all-wise court were that the hobo should go to the State Penitentiary for 20 years, while the cold-blooded murderer was sent to prison for two years. And the sentences stood.

This was in accordance with the traditions inherited from the old Vigilantes, who were bound together under this oath:

> "We, the undersigned, uniting ourselves together for the laudable purpose of arresting thieves and murderers and recovering stolen property, do hereby pledge ourselves on our sacred honor, each to all others, and solemnly swear that we will reveal no secrets, violate no laws of right, and never desert our standard of justice, so help us God."

And the first of the Vigilante bylaws was: "The only punishment that shall be inflicted by this committee is death."

Fifteen years later, when the Vigilantes were called on again to straighten things out, this section was amended to provide banishment from the camp for any tricky business.

Up to the beginning of the present century there had been but one legal hanging in Butte, with all of its murders. It is only fair to say, however, that in the long list of first degree crimes, there was not a single murder that had robbery as its purpose. Most of them occurred in open and more or less fair fights between bad men or in settlement of personal feuds, in which the ready six-shooter was the first resort, as well as the last. And, in compliance with the unwritten law of the land, there were very few cases in which a man was shot from ambush or without having been duly warned that he would be "shot at sight." In all such crimes there was little condemnation and few regrets, except among the personal friends of the departed. There was pretty general regret, among both old-timers and newcomers, that both parties to the affair had not been killed instead of only one.

The man who was legally hanged, soon after the incorporation of the town with an original townsite a quarter of a mile square, was much less deserving of that fate than nine out of ten of the killers who received trifling prison terms or were acquitted on the ground of self-defense, which was made to cover a multitude of crimes. With a club as his only weapon, the condemned fellow killed a man in a drunken fight; a few years later there would not have been a chance of convicting him of murder in the first degree, or in any degree, for that matter. But when he came up for trial he practically committed suicide by making no defense, through lack of competent counsel. In those Territorial days, there were few men in the camp who knew anything about law, except the federal judge. Hence there was nothing to do but hang him, a proceeding to which he did not seem greatly opposed. There was a feeling, too, that the young city ought to do something to advertise itself, and no one knew any better way than by a legal execution.

Only one other Butte murder was properly punished, and in that case the verdict was returned in an adjoining county. A young tramp shot a freight conductor who had thrown him off the train on which he was stealing a ride. The conductor had many friends and there was some talk of a lynching party. On the plea that his client could not secure a fair trial at the scene of his crime, the tramp's lawyer applied for, and secured, a change of venue. The case was sent to Boulder County, and the ranchers over there, proud of the distinction accorded them and glad to get their hands on a "bad man" from Butte, hanged him in 10 minutes.

The sentence was carried out in the yard adjoining the county jail and was attended by a fair-sized crowd, though no such throng as would have attended a public execution in an Eastern city. Killings were no great novelty, even in Boulder, in those days, and a hanging in which everything was cut and dried was much less entertaining than a lively shooting scrape. So the attendance at the Boulder fete was comparatively small, though the gates were open to anyone who cared to come in to see the show. Out there the prisoner stands on the ground and is jerked up by a falling weight—at Boulder they used boxes of tin—so the spectators had a good view of the whole proceeding.

When I arrived in Butte, Perry Beal was the coroner, simply by reason of the fact that he was a bullwhacker. He lived in Horse Prairie, which was several miles from the camp and therefore involved considerable delay in cases of suicide or murder. And, like all of the old trail-blazers, Perry drank enough liquor so that he could tell whether it was good or bad, though he didn't often try, and he drank either one with great glee. He had one standard question which he invariably asked every witness to the finding of a body, when someone nudged him at the close of his direct story.

No matter how long the subject of the inquest had been dead, nor the manner of his departure from this life, old Perry would shake himself, stare around for a minute or two until he got his bearings, and then demand to be told: "What, if anything, did the deceased say to you after you found him?" The usual answer, of course, was: "Why, he didn't say anything. He was dead." But by that time, as a rule, Perry was asleep again, and had to be aroused from time to time to continue the questioning. That query was put so often that it finally failed to get a laugh from the regular attendants at inquests.

Things went somewhat better under Judge Muldoon and T.C. Porter, another old bullwhacker who followed him, with John R. Bordeaux as their assistant in fact if not in name. Johnny boasted that he got his education as "shorthand reporter in a livery stable," which must have been true, for it was all he could do to write legibly, though he could spell money right enough. Silver Bow County and Butte were constitutionally short of funds, and Johnny scalped warrants on a basis that netted him about 20 percent. Coroner's fees were at the rate of $1.50 per day, and Johnny paid me $1 or $1.25 of that, depending on how long he would have to wait for his money. But he always paid me in full, which according to his way of figuring, gave him a mortgage on my soul.

The coroner gave me the job of searching the body so I generally got in an extra day. That chore was ordinarily done by a policeman, especially if it was messy, and the cop also took charge of the effects. But I got the fee.

Butte was always in such a hurry that several times there was such a mad rush to call the coroner that Johnny was there before the man or woman died, or close behind. Morphine—which could be bought openly in any amount—was the favorite way of going out by suicide. Three or four times Johnny arrived to find me walking the patient up and down or beating him with wet towels to keep him with us a while longer. After staying around a while and surveying the scene in order to hazard a guess as to the probable outcome, Johnny would begin begging me to "come on and let him die, so we can go home."

His plaintive and pathetic appeals always went unheeded, and in at least two cases we pulled the patient through. And the attempt was not renewed, I believe. For it often happened that the morphine was taken as a result of too much barleycorn, and the man or woman repented of it when rationality was restored.

One night a man was taken to the city jail in the belief that he was dead drunk. There it was discovered by the city physician that he had taken morphine, and the doctor thought there was a chance of saving him if we kept him walking. So Frank Anderson, who was on night duty at the time, and I took him in hand and started the parade. In the meantime Judge Muldoon arrived, with Johnny in attendance. Both were annoyed at what they saw, for they had been dragged out of bed. Johnny was particularly distressed. After watching the walking match for a few minutes he joined it and, walking beside me, said in a voice that was filled with tears:

"Go ahead and let the man die. He wanted to die or he wouldn't have taken the stuff. I always pay you full value for your warrants, anyway. Come on, be a good fellow, and let him die, so we can get back to bed."

But I could not hear very well that night, and the parade continued. And the man did not walk "the last mile," but came back from the great beyond, and was glad to have taken the long walk, though his shoulders were sore from the beating we gave him.

Late one night Tom Porter received word that a miner's wife living away out west of Missoula Gulch had cut her throat and become a case for the coroner, and I rode with him in the dead wagon. We reached the scene to find the report slightly exaggerated. The woman had cut her throat, rightly enough, and had made a pretty good job of it. She was lying out in the woodshed in a great pool of blood. But she was still alive, though she had completely severed the windpipe and, from the looks of the wound, she could not long survive. Tom and I sat down in the front room, with the "distracted" husband, and waited for the end. But it was not her time to die, and after waiting for half an hour or more, I said if she lived 15 minutes longer I was going to take her to Witherspoon's hospital and see if the doctor could not patch her up.

Witherspoon was the best surgeon in Butte, or in Montana, and I had helped him get started when he landed in the camp about the same time that I did. The city physician took his own time in responding to emergency calls, and whenever I got to an attempted suicide and found no doctor there, I told the cops to send for Witherspoon.

"Who's Witherspoon?" they asked, at first.

"A young doctor up on Broadway. He's the best doctor in Butte, too, if that makes any difference," I told them.

Witherspoon came on the jump, and if the chances were anywhere near even, he'd pull a suffering person through—for all of which I gladly gave him credit. Then his fame began to spread, and before long he had a hospital of his own and the biggest practice in Butte.

The woman was still alive when the time limit expired so we loaded her in the dead wagon, took her to the hospital, dug Witherspoon from bed and left her. He said the next day that if we had waited another quarter of an hour it would have been too late. By putting her on the operating table in such a position that the blood all ran to her head, he sewed up the windpipe and the ghastly looking wound in her throat and he thought she would recover. Which she did—and left her husband when she left the hospital.

Such were the ways of the coroners and Johnny Bordeaux in the "greatest mining camp on earth!"

WHEN REPORTERS NEEDED SIX-SHOOTERS

There was one particular day that an array of Butte was threatened. There were guns aplenty—more of them, in fact, than on any other day except holidays—but "one side was afraid and the other dassent." This fact and a kindly providence alone prevented the camp from being made a shambles.

That was on July 4th, 1894, the day of the American Protective Association and the Roman Catholic riots. The APA had grown steadily but silently until it attained such strength that it had grabbed the preceding county election, lock, stock and barrel, to the great surprise of everybody except themselves. The Catholics could see, without the aid of any binoculars, that if their enemies stuck together in the same fashion, they could win the city election in the fall just as easily. Therefore the relations between the Protestants and the Catholics, who ordinarily dwelt together in harmony, became badly strained. There were frequent fights between the Irish and Cousin Jacks and, as it turned out, both sides were making preparations for the Glorious Fourth. Almost everybody's number was up, and the lines were sharply drawn.

I gained my first intimation of the coming war from Sergeant Ed Carroll, of the police force, as we were making the rounds a few days before the Fourth.

"There's going to be hell here on the Fourth," he said, grimly. "The APAs are going to start it and we are going to finish it. I've got my plans all made. I've got a big butcher knife sharpened to a razor edge on both sides, and I'm going to mix with the mob and cut the guts out of a bunch of 'em. Being a police officer, I'll never be suspected and I can get a lot of 'em in the scrap. The undertakers will be burying APAs for weeks."

"Let me tell you something, Ed," I said. "It's damned bad business for a policeman to be plotting wholesale murder, even if he is a Catholic and the APAs are on the other side. But it shows rotten judgment on your part to be telling in advance what you are planning to do. You know I don't talk, but if the fight does come off, you'll be about the first one to stop a bullet."

"Not on your life. I'm not talking much about what I'm going to do but I'm getting ready just the same," he said.

"If you are talking like that to me, a Protestant, you're talking about it enough that the APAs will hear of it. If I were you and were plotting a general murder, I'd keep my mouth sealed until the blowoff."

In that guess I was right, for Carroll was so constituted that with a battle looming, and a religious battle at that, he could not remain silent. I said nothing about his plans, one reason being that I thought Ed was simply talking to make conversation, as he had a habit of doing. But as events proved, he must have told others of his scheme.

Hell With the Lid Off

My room then was on Broadway, midway of the block between Main and Academy Streets. Simon Hauswirth's saloon was to the left, toward Main Street, and Thomas & Tickell's saloon was near Academy Street, to the right. They were the APA headquarters. In their decorations for the Fourth, both places flaunted their colors to the world, in an evident desire to provoke hostilities. Hauswirth arranged medium-sized American flags in a gigantic APA over his windows and the door, and Thomas & Tickell's made a similar display, with smaller flags, over the entrance. The windows of Hauswirth's saloon were of the ordinary size, in a business block, but those at the Sazerac were large and wide.

Just after I had gone to my room, soon after 3 o'clock in the morning, a little Irishman placed a stick of dynamite on the front sill of one of Hauswirth's windows, put a brick over it and set it off. It made quite a racket, but, though not being confined, did little damage beyond smashing the glass and breaking some bottled goods that were displayed in the window. But it was the signal for the gathering of the clans.

As it was too late to get a story in the paper that night, I turned in, to be awakened about 9 o'clock by noises in the street. Going to the window I found Broadway solidly packed with people, with the crowds a little denser if that were possible in front of Hauswirth's saloon and Thomas & Tickell's. I found out later that orders had been issued to the APAs to stay on the outside of all crowds and fire into them as rapidly as they could. But the crowds were so thick that all orders were off that day. The APAs and Catholics were side by side, and about every man had a gun in his pocket and his hand on it. Those who were not armed carried clubs and brickbats.

I looked around for Carroll and finally spotted his red hair. He evidently had not yet begun operations with his butcher knife, for the people were so tightly packed around him it would be difficult for him to circulate with any freedom. Then I noticed a fellow who I knew quite well gradually working his way toward Carroll from the rear. From his stealthy approach and the way he kept quietly advancing I suspected that he had something more on his mind than his hat. The distance was too great for me to call out a warning to Carroll, making my voice heard above the ceaseless din of the mass of people. So all I could do was watch.

When the fellow got right behind Carroll he fired from his coat pocket. He aimed for his heart, but either aimed too high or the crowd interfered with his marksmanship, for the bullet just nipped Ed's shoulder. Immediately Ed forgot all about his plans and took it on the run for parts unknown. It would have seemed impossible for a man to force his way through the thickly packed mob on the run, but Carroll did just that, throwing people to the right and left, and he was not seen again until late that night, when the excitement was all over.

My attention landed on Dennis Daly, a somewhat violent Irish member of the police force who was haranguing the crowd as he sought to clear a path to remove a man he was taking into custody. In the window just above and a little to his right, a room occupied by two very good friends of mine, there was a suspicious movement of the lace curtains. While I looked, the curtains were drawn back a trifle at the side and there was a puff of smoke. Daly went down, with a bullet through his heart. No one went upstairs to make any inquiry as to who fired the shot. The Irish seemed afraid and the APAs knew, or didn't know, and nor did they care. They were too much occupied with things directly around them.

It was out of the question for the dead wagon to force its way through the crowd, so Daly was carried to a side street and taken away to the Irish undertaker. The coroner was an APA, and the verdict was, in the words of one of the jury, that "Daly came to his death at the hands of parties unknown." He was the only man who was killed, and no effort was made to ascertain the identity of his slayer.

Thinking the killing of Daly might prove the match that would set off the fireworks, I decided to get on the outside as quickly as possible. The first thing I did, being short of cartridges for my gun and having many friends and some enemies in both camps, was visit Wehl's firearms shop and buy a box of .45s. Five minutes later the police closed the store. Then, prepared for anything that might happen, I joined the mob.

Instead of having the effect I feared, the slaying of Daly exerted an opposite influence, on the surface at least. It put something of a quietus on the Catholics, at the same time making them more sullen, and it steadied the APAs. The police were busy arresting APAs, and deputy sheriffs were equally busy arresting Catholics and putting them behind the bars of the city or county jail. This no doubt kept down the killings, for the most strenuous voiced agitators, on both sides, were quickly locked up.

At about the time Daly died, the street narrowly escaped being turned into a slaughterhouse. Sheriff Sam Reynolds and Billy Young, the undersheriff, and two others came up from the basement of Thomas & Tickell's, each with two double-barreled shotguns, leaded almost to the muzzle with buckshot, intending to empty them through the front windows and then make it appear that the place had been attacked. But someone with sense thought to pull aside the shades which were closely drawn and look out. He saw, and recognized, a number of APAs, so they held their fire. The APAs had been told to keep away from the front of the saloon but some of them had been caught in the jam and carried there and then could not get out. And not all of them had received the instructions. But for this fact the guns might well have been emptied into the mob, and columns in the papers the next day would have been filled with the list of dead.

The Fire Department was called out to throw water on the crowds, but in half a minute the hose was cut and rendered useless. Then Mayor Dugan and John J. McHatton, the leaders of the Catholics, and prominent APAs spoke to the mob, begging them to go home. All were ridiculed. Even Rabbi Maurice Eisenberg was howled down. Soon the militia arrived and the town was put under martial law.

Then came another surprise. Butte had three companies in the National Guard and one of them, composed entirely of Irishmen, was known as the "Meagher Guards." The APAs and their adherents dreaded the appearance of the Guards, on account of their reputation, with all due respect for military discipline. Hence they were greatly relieved, and as much surprised, when but a handful of them turned out. It was reported that Charley Gardner, captain of the guards, was an Orangeman, and that his first lieutenant and many members of the company were of the same faith. This news, added to the death of Officer Daly, was about all the Catholics could stand, and they milled around all night, in their own saloons, while the APAs drank all they could hold, and often more.

But the militia restored order, in jig time, after 12 hours of turmoil. The next day the camp was quiet and the soldiers were withdrawn. When the time came for nominations for the city administration the APAs put a straight ticket in the field, headed by William Thompson, popularly known as "Old Bill," for mayor. He had come down from Virginia City, and would tackle his weight in wildcats any day for a principle. He was short, bow-legged and had a squeaky voice. He was meek and mild in manner and did not express his opinions under ordinary conditions. But when he was asked for his views he came right out in meeting and gave voice to them plainly, whether he was among friends or enemies.

There was a strong Missouri colony in Butte, headed by G.W. Stapleton, himself an old Vigilante, which about everybody kowtowed to politically. But not Old Bill, who had run afoul of the Missourians in Alder Gulch and knew all about them, in a way that was satisfactory to him. He ran a mill down near the old placer diggings and one day wanted a gang of men. So he had a sign painted, with letters six feet high, reading:

20 MEN WANTED FOR TIMBER CUTTING. NO MISSOURIANS OR CHINAMEN NEED APPLY

It showed what he thought of Missourians, and it was the talk of the town for a week. Almost everybody on his side of the fence wanted Old Bill to run, except himself. At last some smart politician told him the Missourians were anxious for him to make the race so that they could knife him.

"Oh they do, do they?" he said. "They're talking that way eh? Well, I'll be jiggered. All right! I'll run then to give them a chance to use the knife."

Bill led his ticket, and was elected by such a big majority that the Missourians cut much less of a figure in the subsequent elections. Right after his election I had Archie McMillan, who was to be the new city clerk, make an appointment for me to see him in the evening. The old man got right down to brass tacks.

"Well, what do you want to see me about? You're on the other side of the fence," he said.

"Maybe I am and maybe I'm not, but if you think I'm a Catholic because I'm working on Mr. Daly's paper, you're crazy," I told him. "I want to see you about your chief of police."

"Well, what do you want?"

I told him I wanted him to name a man chief of police.

Old Bill almost jumped out of his seat. "Oh, by sorry, NO. He's a Missouri sonnykabick. I won't do it. No."

"He's a Missourian all right, but he's not a sonnykabick. And he is the only Protestant on the force. He's the natural man for the place and you've got to appoint him."

"Got to, eh? Well, I won't name any Missourian for that post, or any other. That's all there is to that."

However, I gradually won the old man over, and before we parted he had agreed to name my choice. We parted good friends, of the kind that are made in the West in one talk, and we became closer as time went by. We kept the news about the appointment to ourselves and other candidates for the office got all heated up in the race. But Thompson's word was good enough for me, as it was for anyone else who knew him. He created a mild sensation by naming a Missourian for chief of police of Butte. But the chief stayed away from the Missouri clique.

There was only one suggestion that the old Vigilantes might get together again for the purpose of cleaning up Butte—in fact, there was but once when there was any need of them—and it was amazing to see the results. During the semi-panic of 1897, the camp was the most prosperous city in the country with no scarcity of either work or money. This was commented on in the newspapers, and tough characters descended on the town in droves, from all parts of the country. Hold-ups, which had been practically unknown before, were of almost nightly occurrence. The police seemed powerless before the assembled multitude of gangsters.

I proposed to Mayor Bill Thompson, who had participated in the early-day hanging of Sheriff Henry Plummer and his band of road agents at Virginia City, that any of the old Vigilantes still living take the situation in hand. The mayor demurred. He didn't think conditions were bad enough to justify retribution of that kind.

"No, I don't think we are needed," he said. "There hasn't been a single robbery with murder. If that comes, and the police can do nothing about it, we may take a hand. But, he added, "if you want to print a story saying that we are thinking about it, it can't do any harm, and it might do some good, maybe. I'll see that the story is not denied."

Accordingly, the Standard the next morning carried a story in which it was stated that the old stranglers were "thinking seriously" of getting out their ropes and cleaning up Butte as the Vigilance Committee cleaned up Alder Gulch in the old days. During the night I backed this up by marking the old Vigilante sign 3-7-77, with chalk on the sidewalks at strategic points throughout the town.

Those cabalistic figures were supposed to represent a grave three feet wide, seven feet long and 77 inches deep. That day and for two days following, every freight train that left Butte was crowded to the guards with tough hombres of all grades. There were so many of them, and they were all in such a hurry to get away, that the train crews soon tired of trying to kick them off the cars on which they had taken refuge. In 72 hours there was not a strange bad man left in the camp.

Their departure, in a panic, was a tribute to the fame of the Vigilantes. Though they had been idle for more than 30 years, the mere intimation that they "might" go into business again terrified every man in the biggest gang of desperadoes Butte had ever seen. If the Vigilantes had seriously considered any renewed activity, there would have been no publicity about it, of course. But the bad men from the outside did not know that. And they did not stay long enough to ask any questions.

Racehorse "Spokane"

CHAPTER 13
THE SPORTING LIFE

Scoundrels in the sport of "copper" kings

The Butte football team won the game, of course, and the list of casualties on the San Francisco team was quite ghastly

The race courses built in Butte and Anaconda by Marcus Daly were complete to the last notch, like everything else he did. The one at Butte, which had a seating capacity of 20,000, rose from the barren waste of the flat south of the camp like a blot on the face of the moon, while the one at Anaconda, with a capacity half as large, was next door to the Garden of Eden. It had flowers and trees and grass all around it, while little wisps of bunch grass was all that could withstand the smelter smoke of Butte.

Race meetings of 30 days were held in both towns, beginning with Butte, and they were largely patronized. The few good women in the camp attended in small parties, and the sporting ladies were out in force. For them, it was the event of the year, the one time when they could put on their fine clothes and go out en masse. Yet so great was the camp's respect for women, good or bad, that when they showed themselves in public they never were annoyed or insulted.

Their dresses, on which some of them had been busy for weeks, were the last word in the art of attire and though perfectly respectable, they rendered them easily recognizable. But that was the only thing about them that indicated their calling, for many of them vied with the wives of my superintendents and foremen in seeming respectability.

The space under the grandstand for almost its entire length was devoted to the bar, on which mining pioneer Miles Finlen had a life-time lease—with no return to the owner. Finlen occupied a high chair, midway of the bar, from which he could survey the whole scene. All gold pieces were brought to him for change and he dropped them behind a semi-circular pile of silver dollars against the back bar. Every afternoon he would have a heap of gold representing thousands of dollars.

The V-shaped space under the last rows of seats, leading down to the ground, was ordinarily used by a florist. One day it was unoccupied, with the door swinging open, and it struck me that any man with a little nerve would find it a simple matter to step inside, pull the door shut, cut a hole through the back bar, which was full of cracks, and walk off with all the gold pieces. And that is exactly what some smart crook did just a few days later. Miles let out a yell that was heard as far away as Helena, and a quick search was made for the missing yellow coins, and the man who had them. But it was in vain.

The betting ring, off to the left of the stand, was given up largely to parimutuel boxes, in which the smallest bet that could be made was $5. Auction pools were sold at a Butte hotel the night before and at the track in advance of every race, and these got some play. But there was very little book betting because the public liked to make its own odds. Bookmakers from the East tried it a couple of times but got such a light play that they gave it up. Sam Martin, a local product, tried it intermittently but he always had a sponge in one hand and a piece of chalk in the other, and a $10 bet would cause a change in the odds right down the line. So he did not get much of a play.

The bulk of the betting was in the mutuel boxes, and a large part of it was done by women, good and bad alike. The less respectable ladies were put in on good things by friends among the horsemen. There were a few touts, but not nearly so many as circulated on the Eastern tracks. The men of the mines were a cagey lot and they much preferred playing their own judgment to taking a tip from a tout. Furthermore, when a tip went wrong, the tout stood an excellent chance of being put out of commission for several days by the fists of the victim. After two or three examples had been made of misguided touts, the business went into a decline.

In Butte, attendance was always large and often overflowed the grandstand. The purses were of good size and the attendance of Eastern horsemen, with their horses, with two months of good racing at the end of the route, was substantial. Daly, naturally, did not race his horses. But he was a frequent attendant at the Butte meeting and was at the track in Anaconda almost every day. A certain number of miners were let off every day to attend the races, and it did not require the attendance of the shift bosses to see that they kept faith. Many who were off shift at the time were also there, and all of them brought their pocketbooks.

When the tracks were in charge of local men, fixes were put over quite frequently, and horses were "shooed in" that had no right to win. But in 1895, Mr. Daly imported highly regarded Edward A. Tipton, of Lexington, Kentucky, to run both tracks. Shady ways ceased and money began going into the grandstand, for a change. Then Tipton brought out P.P. "Prickly Pear" Johnston as presiding judge and then they stopped entirely. Thereupon the number of Eastern stables, with the prospect of two months of square racing, increased perceptibly. Judge Johnston, a genial, kindly soul, could smell a job a mile away and he had a habit of calling off all bets on the slightest suspicion. That quickly broke the bad actors of their crooked ways.

Old By Holly was one man who took no chances on losing a race by having his horse held back. Every time he had a horse entered where he thought he ought to win and had a good bet down, he would warn the jockey that he would be at the head of the home stretch with a shotgun, and that he would shoot him off the horse if he didn't come into the straightaway with a good lead.

"This horse can win if he's ridden right," he would say, "and I'm going to make sure that he is ridden that way. If he comes into the stretch in the lead, nothing can beat him, so you ride him that way. If you don't I'll shoot you off him."

Under such plain instructions, Holly's entry was ridden to perfection and every time old By was at the head of the stretch when his horse won. It finally got so that every time I saw By wandering off to the head of the stretch I hurried to get a bet down on his horse.

The Butte track was one of the fastest in the country and for years held the world's record for a quarter of a mile dash. One day, when I had been thrown off my horse, figuratively speaking, and rolled over, I made up my mind that I would pick out a dog on which no tickets had been sold and get all of the money in the box or go broke. It was the last race of the day, a half-mile dash for three-year olds who hadn't won a race that year. It was filled with animals that threatened to jump the fence every time they saw a bone in the infield. When they went to the post, I dropped down to survey the mutual boxes.

There was one ungainly looking brute on which not a ticket had been sold, and, waiting until the last minute, as I thought, I bought one ticket on him. I expected that I would rake in the pot if he won but I overlooked the fact that some people thought I had some inside information about the race and followed my lead. Right behind me five or six people bought tickets on the same horse. The brute must have been feeling his oats for he won by about a hundred yards. The tickets paid something over $4,000, at that, so I was good and even on the day.

There were five thoroughbred races every day and one harness race; not that Daly or the public wanted them but some of the horse owners did, and Daly had some good friends among them. So the harness races were a fixture. Charley Hoffman of Bozeman owned a black mare named Vollula which figured in them, though she wasn't often bracketed.

Charles H. Eggleston, associate editor of the Standard, had a queer but sometimes very keen sense of humor. He sat in on the wire from Butte on one or two nights a week. One night there was some confusion over the name of Vollula, which in some way became involved. Johnny Dierks, the operator at the Anaconda end of the wire, broke in to inquire about it and Bob Curran, our operator, asked me. I told him, over my shoulder, to tell them to "make 'em all Vollula," and he sent it just that way.

That struck Egg as funny, somehow, and he let it stand in the story and for several weeks thereafter, whenever he was handling the Butte news, he would insert it in the most ridiculous places. It did not trouble me at all, though more than once I was called on for an explanation, which was freely given. Once it was stated in a church story that "Bishop Soandso, of the Methodist Church, who had been in Butte for several days, attending to Church affairs, and making 'em all Vollula, had returned to Helena." Everyone on the paper thought it was a good joke, and typical of Egg. But not Hoffman. He finally went right to Old Man Daly.

"What the devil is your paper trying to do with that mare of mine, Vollula?" he asked, in some heat. "She's a damned good mare and the Standard is making fun of her." The fun-making stopped.

All of which goes to show what a fine time we had on the Standard.

A REALITY THAT ANYBODY COULD STRIKE IT RICH

One of the oddities about life in the far West was the camp's water supply. It came from the eternally snow-clad hills across the flat, about 10 miles south of the city, which, subsequently, when the water became civilized, was a favorite place for picnic parties. The altitude there was considerably higher than Butte and people were sure to find plenty of snow, even in midsummer, with a bright sun overhead. But for two or three years it was visited only by men who were obliged to go there, and they had to have either good stomachs or weak noses, or both.

The trouble was with the reservoir. When it was enlarged to keep up with the increasing demand for water for cooking purposes, the trees were simply cut down and the whole mass of accumulated messy muck, as it became as soon as it was inundated, was left. The result was that the water smelled to high heaven and Eugene Carroll, the general manager for the water company, was the most unpopular man in the camp. The water actually gave off such a stench that when the watering carts passed, people felt obliged to put their handkerchiefs to their noses.

One morning I printed a story—on somewhat doubtful authority, it must be admitted—that it was reported that a badly decomposed Chinaman had been taken from the reservoir, and the camp was in an uproar. The odor of the water was very much like that of a decaying cadaver, and the story had all the semblance of truth. The tale was promptly denied, of course, but Carroll had to sneak in and out of his office and keep the door locked for two days. As a matter of fact, it never was fully established that there was a body in the reservoir, but there might have been a dozen, from the smell of the water. One summer it got so bad that sprinkling carts were not permitted on some of the streets.

In consequence, ranchers took advantage of the city's dilemma and water taken from mountain streams, which had no odor, was peddled through the camp and sold for 10 cents a bucket. This went on for two or three years, though the offensive smell was much more noticeable in summer than in winter. The wagons for the mountain water were specially built, and they did a rushing business. Butte was the only city of which I ever heard that had water that smelled so bad.

Hell With the Lid Off

Frederick Mueller discovered copper precipitation by the use of tin cans and scrap iron, but made little use of it, though he secured a three-year lease on water from the Anaconda mine. It remained for Jim Ledford to make a similar find and capitalize on it. Ledford lived in a cabin in Dublin Gulch, which he moved into when he came from the Black Hills. He had the reputation of working when he had to and loafing the rest of the time.

His backyard, like practically all of the yards in the camp, had a large accumulation of tin cans. There had been a fire in the St. Lawrence mine that never could be put out, and the water that seeped out and ran through Ledford's back yard was heavily impregnated with copper. One spring morning, Jim noticed that the cans had disappeared. In their place was a molten mass, which he suspected was valuable. He had it assayed, and it proved to be almost pure copper, the water having eaten away the tin and deposited the richer metal in its place.

Ledford hustled downtown and secured a year's lease on the water from the St. Lawrence. He built a succession of great wooden tanks, enlarging the system rapidly as his revenue increased, the water running through them, from one to the other, until all of the copper was extracted. In two months there was not an empty tin can in Butte; in six months there were none in Montana. The discovery, therefore, served a good purpose, in addition to making about $100,000 for Ledford, before the company took over the lease, on Sept. 1st, 1896. The Anaconda hill is now covered with boxes into which water from the mines is pumped. Nothing that is worthwhile gets away from the company in these modern days.

That was one reason why all of the men who were white clear through were treated alike in Butte—because the man who was down on his luck today might strike it rich tomorrow. Ledford was about the last man in the world who could be considered lucky, but when his chance came he saw it and seized it. And the camp was dotted with mines that carried a suggestion, and often more, of romance.

The Wake up Jim mine, of the Anaconda Company, was located by Jim Toohey and another old prospector in the early days. They were searching the Anaconda hill for specimens of silver or copper ore, but had found nothing encouraging when night arrived. They camped on the ground, and over night there was a very light fall of snow. In the morning Jim's partner got up and set the coffee to boiling. Jim was a sound sleeper and after his partner had called him a couple of times he gently kicked him in the ribs and said "Wake up, Jim." His heel struck a piece of rock and turned it over—and it did not require trained eyes to see, against the white background, that it was rich in copper. They were so excited that they located the claim before breakfast, giving it the name by which it was discovered. Later on they sold it to Daly, and it became one of the big producers of the Anaconda Company.

One day two Swedes got off the cable-train at the end of the line in Walkerville as I was about to get on. They had not been in the country long enough to speak very good English but they said they wanted to mine. They carried picks and shovels and, in the supposition that they were looking for jobs, I directed them to the Alice Mine office. But they said they did not want to work for anybody but themselves, and inquired where was a good place to start.

"Ore is where you find it," I said, "and you are likely to find it anywhere around here. That's a good place, over there."

I pointed to a section of open ground near the end of the cable road. They took me at my word and went to work and soon uncovered a nice vein of silver ore. Then they proved that they were wise in the ways of mining, for they found that they were on an unlocated fraction, which they at once took up, and sold their discovery for $20,000.

But these strikes of fortune were not the real reason why all men who were men were treated on the same basis. It was because the people of the camp had not been spoiled by contact with Easterners and retained all of the natural warmth and generosity and kindliness with which they were born.

Reading from left to right, top row: Jack Monroe, Bob Ellis, Bob Weiss, Wallace Perham, Charley Hooper, W. P. Langley. Middle row: Chet Smith, D. N. Richards, D. Gay Stivers (manager), Bill Slater, George "Snake" King. Bottom row: W. McPherson, W. B. Laswell, Francis Brooks, Don Gillis and Wilbur Boyce. Jim Hooper, John V. Bohn, J. J. Hartzell, George McMillan and some other members of the squad were not present when this picture was taken.

MINERS TO THE GRIDIRON

Butte went plumb football crazy in 1893 and 1894. Until injuries took their toll, the Butte Pastime Athletic Club was a corking team, thanks to the generosity of Marcus Daly, who gave a good job doing not much of anything to every man who was vouched for by the manager, DeGay Stivers, a young man with a passion for wearing women's silk stockings. Donald Gillis was quarterback, and a more brilliant player than he was did not walk in the West. Tom and Wilbur Boyce were up in the line, and Johnny Bohn, a little cyclone who had coached at Cornell, was an end. George "Snake" King, a giant from an Eastern university, was a tackle. Some idea of the individual size of the club may be gained from the fact that Jack Munroe, the prizefighter known to the other players as "Shagnasty," the muscled fellow who would defeat heavyweight champion Jim Jeffries in an exhibition, was a substitute.

In 1894, we went to California to play the Reliance Athletic Club on Christmas Day and the Olympic Athletic Club on New Year's Day, and I went along, just to keep them company. We made the trip in the Minnewaska, a beautiful hotel car of the Northern Pacific, and stopped off en route to play Seattle and Portland, which was just like shooting fish. Arriving in San Francisco, we were the guests of the Olympic Club and I got off on the wrong foot by bawling out the Sons of the Golden West, of which the Californians were very proud in those days but of whom the Butte crowd thought a little less than nothing. I did not know that the man who visited us at our car was a reporter for the San Francisco Examiner. After my apology, everything was lovely.

The managers of the Reliance and Olympic teams had both sworn, when the games were arranged, that they would play only members of their clubs. But, after looking our boys over, and especially after taking several looks at Munroe, the "Fighting Butte Miner," that pledge was openly violated. Our Jim Thompson had attended Princeton University and had a sweater with a big P on it. It was the year Princeton had a star guard who had covered himself in glory. So we put Thompson's sweater on Shagnasty and told him not to tell anyone the time of day, for the minute he opened his mouth we knew the sluff would be off. For several days Shagnasty remembered his orders, and the people were literally standing on their heads with excitement. Then one day he forgot himself and opened his mouth. The ruse was over, but it was good while it lasted.

Reliance beat us. They played clean football and our boys had no excuses, except that they were not good enough to win. Then came the Olympic team, which had even more outsiders on it, including the stars of two or three universities. They made the mistake of starting the rough stuff. Our team never played rough except when they were encouraged to. But when the other side started it, the Butte team always finished it.

Hell With the Lid Off

Gillis came out of a scrimmage with a broken arm, and after that they were busy carrying off members of the Olympic team. We won the game, of course, and the list of casualties on the other side was quite ghastly.

Then the Southern Pacific Railroad offered to transport teams to Santa Barbara free of charge if we would play an All-California team. Feeling was high and the railroad figured that it would break even, and more, by the gate receipts and the fares of people living on their line to wherever it was they offered to take us. Having already played two all-California elevens, we accepted on the dot. But the football enthusiasts of the "sun-kissed" belt wished to see no more of a team that had put half of the Olympic team in the hospital.

George MacMillan, who had played professional football and who managed the Reliance team; George B. Dygert, who had played for the University of Michigan and whom we picked up in San Francisco; and W.B. Lasswell, a famous linebacker from Portland; were so entranced with the ways of the Butte team that they came back with us. We were then arranging to challenge the winner of the Yale-Harvard game when Yale coach Walter Camp came out to look us over. He blew the roof off by charges that our team had professionals, not amateurs, which was true. After that, for want of competition, interest in football in Butte waned badly.

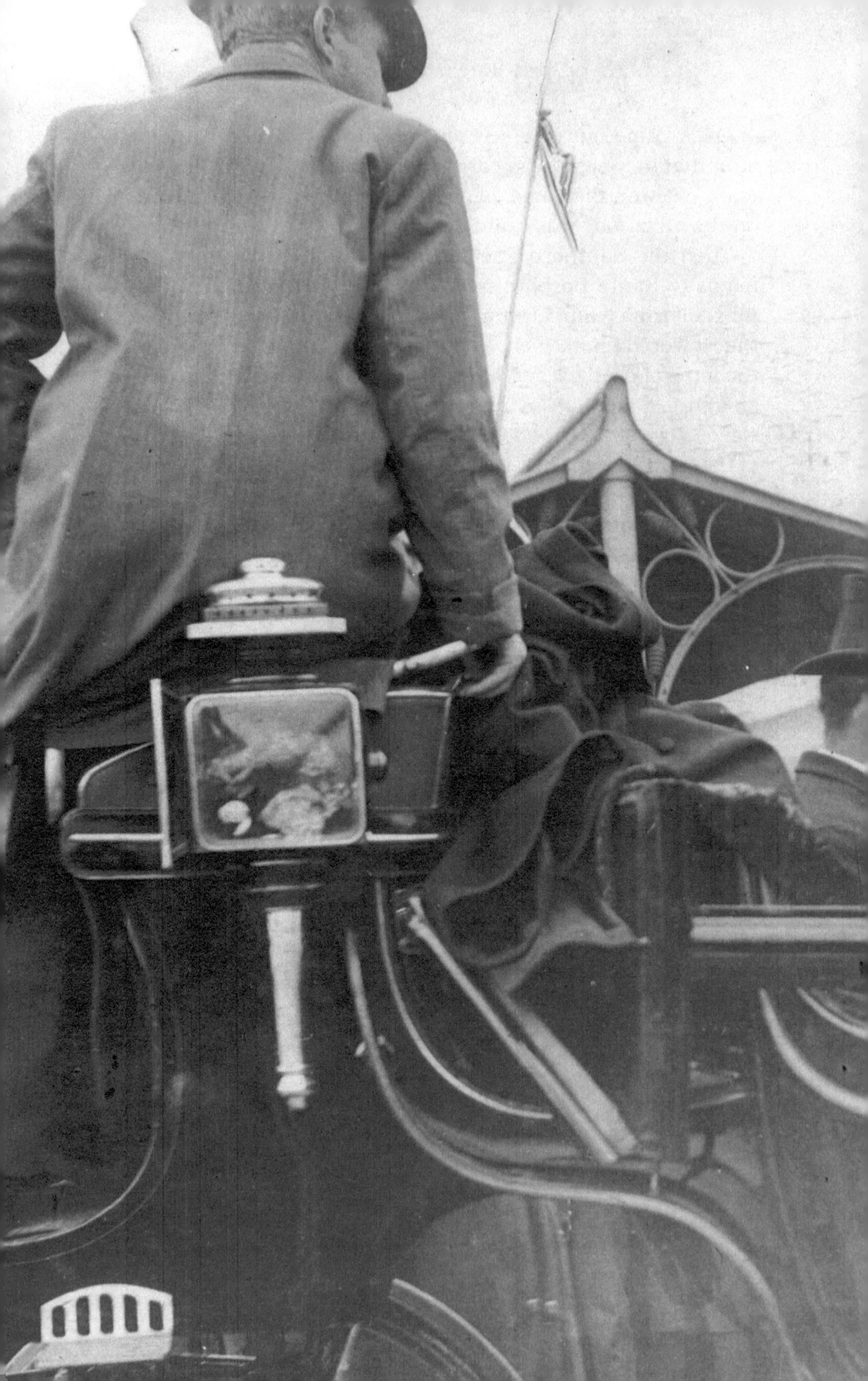

CHAPTER 14
A MEASURE OF BUTTE'S MEN

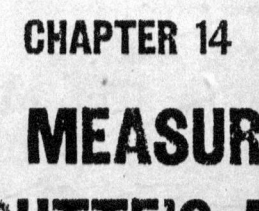

Litigious Jim Murray, Fat Jack Jones, and a cavalcade of characters

President Roosevelt yelled "faster, faster Jack" until the horses were galloping madly

There were men in Butte who had been there so long that they were regarded more as institutions than individuals. Jim Murray was one of them. Jim, who was Canadian-born, drifted into the placer mining camp in 1868 and liked it so well that he never left. He made money in all sorts of ways, as one will sometimes do in a camp that is successively a placer camp, a silver camp and a copper camp, until he had enough to establish a private bank, under his own name of James A. Murray.

But he was above all else a gambler, not with cards—though he liked them, too—but with individuals and real estate. And he was a professed, professional and untiring litigant. He enjoyed nothing quite so much as winning a lawsuit, though it might be for only $1,000. And he kept one large law firm fairly busy with his transactions. Whenever there was an opportunity, he carried his cases to the United States Supreme Court, and for years his name appeared on the docket of that tribunal more often than that of any other man or firm. Every decision in his favor, no matter what the amount involved, was hailed with glee and made the excuse for a celebration, to which the loser was invited more often than not. If he accepted he would have to sit through a long dinner, on which no expense was spared, and listen to good-natured taunts from the winner. And, if possible, he would be badgered into another speculation.

Murray was also the unofficial measurer for the camp. He generally carried a tape measure and a piece of string in his pocket with which he would quietly, and very un-ostentatiously, get the size of anything on which he might make a bet. That would make the bet a sure thing, of course, when nature was allowed to take its course. But Jim did not object at all to the other party taking similar measurements and betting on them. He only hoped he would catch him at it. One bet of this kind brought him up against a loss one day. He had taken the height of a hitching post in Front of Ernest Lange's and, as he and the politician Lee Mantle and some other friends were entering the saloon, Murray paused at the door, sized up the post and remarked:

"Lee, I'll bet you $500 that I can guess the height of that post closer than you can."

Mantle apparently did not hear him, and went on into the saloon with the others. But he knew that Murray had measured the post and in a few minutes he went into the back room, where he found the swamper, cleaning up.

"I wish you would go out in front and drive that post about six inches into the ground," said Mantle. "But don't let anyone inside see you doing it, and say nothing about it."

While they were drinking the porter sent out, without any of them paying any attention to him, and obeyed instructions. Eventually Murray and his friends had all the liquor they needed and left the place. As they reached the sidewalk, and the hitching post loomed in front of them, Mantle said:

"Oh, there's that post. You said something about it, Jim. What was it?"

"I offered to bet you $500 that I can guess closer to the height of it than you can."

"Well, that strikes me as a reasonable proposition," replied Mantle. "I'll go you on that. Not that the height of a hitching post is really important but it's interesting, from that point of view." He started to walk closer to the post, as though he proposed to gauge the height of it from his own, but Murray stopped him.

"That doesn't go," he said. "Make your guess from right here, where we are standing."

Jim's guess was exactly the height when he took the measurement, and Mantle, after carefully surveying it, guessed an inch under him. He, of course, won, and they went back into the saloon for more drinks. After the bet had been paid, and Mantle had given $25 to the swamper, he told Jim how he had won his money. Murray chuckled, and laid new plans for landing Mantle. Lee and Jim fought numerous lawsuits, but continued the best of friends.

It was much the same with Fat Jack Jones, the hackman. Jack, who came to be known to every visitor to the camp from every part of the country, and especially to every prominent visitor, came to Butte just after the War Between the States and drove a hack ever after that until he went to southern California, some years ago, where he was maintained, strange to say, by William A. Clark, Jr., until he died. He is buried there.

Jack got his nickname from the fact that he was considerably more than six feet tall and as thin as a rail. He did more business than any other hackman in the camp; in fact, every man of importance who rode with him once was his client ever after, because of his irreverent intimacy. He was a great friend and admirer of President Theodore Roosevelt, and when the president visited Butte in 1903 he took him on a wild ride across the flat below the camp, after the dinner given him by F.A. Heinze—which the craftiness of John MacGinnis alone prevailed upon the president to attend. Roosevelt called for Fat Jack when the party of four left the hotel, feeling very well, I thank you, and they started for Columbia Gardens, where the President was to make a short speech to some labor unions. But on the way to the Gardens he changed his mind and decided to go for a drive over the flat. It was a wonderful night and wonderful air, which Roosevelt declared would "put new life in an Egyptian mummy." And under the influence of both, he became quite riotous.

The president kept yelling "faster, faster, Jack," until the horses were galloping madly over the flat. With the carriage swaying from side to side in a way that could have thrown him out on his head, he insisted on standing up from time to time and roaring out: "Yippee, this is the life! By Godfrey, this air is great. But speed 'em up a little, Jack." His companions were alarmed by the danger of a catastrophe, but Roosevelt maintained his balance like a sailor in a seaway. And he kept the horses running until his train left.

Jack had good horses because he loved them, and loved to bet on them, which was his financial undoing. There was always racing, and on every race, at some track, Jack had a bet down, if he could finance it. He neglected his business for the races, and during the Butte meeting he was at the track every day. He made frequent loans from Jim Murray, but never paid them back—except once. One of the loans was for $500 with which to buy a new team, for which Jack gave his note. Jim made a trip to Salt Lake City one day and, expecting to return in a few days, he took the note with him. He rode with Jack and at the end of the trip tendered his $500 note in payment. Jack took the piece of paper and looked at it with surprise.

"Oh that..." he said, as he handed it back. "If it's just the same to you, give me 50 cents." Which Murray did.

Jack came to Murray one day in great distress. He wanted $10. "Until tomorrow."

"Nope," said Murray. "I've lent you all of the money I'm going to. Not another cent."

Jack begged, but Jim was adamant. But he relented when, in desperation, Jack offered to pledge his false teeth.

"That's a safe proposition," Jim said. "I can wait for my money as long as you can eat on your gums." And he handed over the ten-spot. But one day's eating without any teeth was all Jack could stand, and he redeemed his teeth.

Jim left a bunch of notes, three inches thick, from men of all grades and all occupations on whom he had made a bet, and which his executors tossed aside as worthless. They totaled into the tens of thousands. But he left about five million dollars in good securities, including in Boulder Springs and Hunter's Hot Springs, on which he had spent hundreds of thousands of dollars, property in California and in Seattle, Tacoma, and Livingston, Montana, plus a lot of real estate in Butte, all of which went to James S. Murray, his nephew, the U.S. Senator from Montana.

THE MANY SALOONS OF JOHN CALHOUN SHEPHERD

Captain John Calhoun Shepherd was another landmark. Where he came from or when he blew into the camp no one ever knew. Some of the old placer miners claimed they found him in a ditch in the diggings below the camp, but that probably was an exaggeration. He had acquired, in some fashion, a Grand Army of the Republic uniform, which he used to substantiate his claim to having been in a War Between the States, though where he had served, or with whom, could not be dragged out of him. The veterans of established reputation in the camp said emphatically he never had been in the war, but Capt. Shepherd simply ignored them. At times, when an effort was made to question him closely, he claimed to have been in the Mexican War, which was too far back to be readily checked up. He was, nonetheless, clean and decent and well educated. He also had a much-practiced cocktail route.

Some of the cocktail places also served food included, so the tail went with the hide. The captain made it a rule to travel his route the first time in the morning, picking up breakfast at the initial stop, and staying long enough in each place for a friendly chat. Then after eight or ten cocktails he would sit down comfortably in the last stopping place and indulge himself in conversation, if there were any intelligent men around or in mediation if there were not. At no place was he asked for money, nor was payment expected; it was just a part of the regular program. In the afternoon he would give the second lap of his route a whirl, stopping in the last place for dinner but being careful not to take breakfast or dinner at the same place more than about once in 10 days. All the exercise he got was in going over his route, and he was not a large eater.

Liquor was the only thing his system seemed to demand, and he could comfortably carry more of that than any other man in the camp. There were about 20 saloons on his route, and he went over it, most of the time, twice a day. During all of the years that I knew him I never saw him even slightly under the influence of liquor more than half a dozen times, and then not enough to make him unsteady on his feet or uncertain in his movements. He was just a shade happier and a little bit more cheerful.

Periods of his over-indulgence in cocktails often preceded the Fourth of July. For all intents and purposes, that was a day set apart for the captain to enjoy himself. He considered and believed he was directly responsible for all of the Fourth of July celebrations in the camp which, if not exactly true, was near enough to satisfy him, and that was the only thing that mattered. Beginning about the middle of June he was almost a nightly visitor at our office, dropping in about 12 or 1 o'clock in the morning and sitting down for an hour or two.

"Well, what are you doing, hey?" he would want to know. "Here the Glorious Fourth is coming on and nobody is doing anything about it, as far as I can see. The people seem to have forgotten about it. Call their attention to it and start the ball rolling."

Then we would write pieces about it, and the captain would come in nearly every night to report progress, though actually the matter was taken out of his hands entirely by the men in charge of the celebration. That, however, made no difference to the captain, as long as something was being done. On the night of July 3 and again on the night of the Fourth, the captain would be attired in all of his regalia, and right in the midst of the celebration, though it was noticeable that he stayed away from the parade. On July 5, he would congratulate the Standard, the mayor and everybody who had a hand in the outpouring of the populace—and then sit back and wait for the next Fourth.

Once the proprietors of his cocktail emporiums chipped in and raised a purse of $1,000, with which they sent the captain East. They outfitted him completely with new clothes and all of the accoutrements and gave him a great send off, with good wishes galore and much liquor, in addition to a bottled supply to keep him company. The old man visited New York and all of the intervening cities, and was back in six or eight weeks, his return being hastened, somewhat, by his inability to build up a cocktail route in the East. He had a collection of wonderful stories, which never ran dry, and he told them, with variations, in all of the places on his route for weeks and months. He complained, particularly, that they did not know what he meant when he ordered a T-bone steak and of their dislike of silver dollars. And he confessed that he did not like their cocktails as well as those that were served at home.

When the captain died, his friends gave him a humdinger of a funeral, with him all dressed up in his Army uniform in the center of it, and with the best band in the camp leading the procession to the cemetery.

THE CHARMED LIFE OF J. BRUCE KREMER

W.M. Tuohy, general agent for the Northern Pacific, was forever playing practical jokes on Major J.E. Dawson, a good-natured old fussbudget who occupied a similar position with Great Northern Railway. The major, when he was going good, must have done something important for his boss, railroad executive James J. Hill, for otherwise he could not have held his job so long. When the Great Northern installed café cars on its trains, the major went all over the town bragging.

Once, Tuohy sent a friend to the major to get a carload rate on post holes.

"Post holes, post holes," sputtered Dawson, "why, you dig post holes, you don't ship 'em."

"That's been true," explained the caller, "but these are just out and patented. You drive 'em in the ground, somehow."

The fact that they were said to have been patented impressed the major, and he wired St. Paul for a rate on them. He received a sarcastic reply from the general freight agent. Another telegram he sent was for a rate on loose hay shipped on flat cars. Similar requests generated inquiries from the general office as to whether he thought he was dealing with fools.

Tuohy had a young brother-in-law, named J. Bruce Kremer, who came out to Butte in 1894 and again in 1896 on vacations from law school. I met him both times and liked him plenty, on account of his way and his natural modesty, which he still has with him. He came back again in 1900 and settled down. He took over Frank E. Corbett's law business, on Corbett's death, and continued to play alone, but successful, up to 1907, when he took his brother, Alfred C. Kremer, and James E. Sanders, a son of Wilbur Fisk Sanders, a territorial pioneer and the old prosecuting attorney for the Vigilantes, into partnership, under the firm name of Kremer, Sanders & Kremer. Like his father, and his partners too, for that matter, Sanders was absolutely without fear, an able man and a good lawyer. That firm continued until Jan. 1 1934, when Sanders retired to become a consulting lawyer, and Alfred Kremer remained in charge of the Butte office.

In 1908, J. Bruce Kremer was elected to the Democratic National Committee, where he remained until the 1930s, when he resigned, expecting to become senator, after having been secretary vice chairman and acting chairman. There never had been much doing nationally until Franklin D. Roosevelt was elected, but up to then Montana has had only two Republican governors—John Ezra Rickards and Joseph Moore Dixon—so that Kremer was always busy with state politics for all of the independents. He played a leading part in litigation over the oil flotation process. An exceptionally wise man, he had sense enough to keep out of the fight in Montana between Heinze and Standard Oil, with the result that he became counsel for all of the independents.

He was an original Roosevelt man and was one of the floor managers at the '32 Democratic National Convention Chicago—the others being Homer S. Cummings and Arthur F. Mullen. After Sen. Thomas J. Walsh declined the attorney generalship, he was prominently mentioned for a place in the Cabinet. But Walsh changed his mind and accepted, then died suddenly just before Roosevelt was inaugurated.

Walsh's death seemingly cleared Kremer's way to the Senate, and Kremer proceeded to Washington. Montana Gov. John E. Erickson had never stated, in so many words, that he would appoint him, but from all that had been said Kremer fully expected to be named. Therefore he was greatly surprised when Erickson resigned and Frank H. Cooney, who succeeded him, appointed the recent governor to the Senate.

That proved to be the luckiest break that Kremer had ever had. He had not recovered from his amazement when he was sought by a large firm, which wished to retain him on a basis much better than that of being a senator. Kremer was told he could live wherever he wished. He suggested Washington, and they acquiesced. Before he got his office

---

Editor's note: In remaining Montana-centric, Smith underplays Walsh's death, though perhaps much of the speculation about the circumstances occurred later. Walsh, a major Democratic player and by most accounts a much-respected senator, on March 3, 1933, 3-3-33, was found dead on the floor of his berth on a train headed for Roosevelt's inauguration and the position of attorney general of the United States. The nation was already awash in political drama with the attempted assassination of FDR, which would take the life of Chicago Mayor Anton Cermak. Five days before his death, Walsh, 73, of Helena, had secretly married Mina Perez Chaumont de Truffin, widow of a Cuban sugar magnate, in Cuba. A day later, FDR announced that Walsh would be his nominee as attorney general. Walsh's death certificate said of the cause: "unknown, possibly coronary thrombosis." No autopsy was done and speculation mounted over the decades that Walsh was poisoned in connection with Cuban political warfare. Before his body returned by train to Montana, saluted along the way, Walsh lay in state in the U.S. Senate—on the day Cermak died.

opened, another big legal firm retained him on an equally extravagant basis. Since then, several other firms have employed him, and he has now reached the point where he is more profitably busy than he ever was in his life, which is saying much, and is turning business away. He is thicker than thieves with President Roosevelt and all of the cabinet and knows every man in Washington who is worth knowing.

A man of keen understanding, far vision, and knowledge of the law from every angle—a man who sees things without the aid of his eyes and feels things without the use of his fingers—J. Bruce Kremer is a man who is going far. And all because Governor Erickson turned him down.

And Erickson himself was turned down by Montana as soon as it got a crack at him.

SOURCE OF GOSSIPY BUTTE SECRETS

One evening a man who gave a name that meant nothing to me called me on the telephone and said he had been making some inquiries and would very much like to have a talk with me. He asked me to call at the McDermott Hotel at 9 o'clock that evening and come right up to his room, the number of which he gave, without being announced. All was very hush and mysterious. But the McDermott was the best hotel in the camp, so I put my gun in my pocket and took a chance.

With my hand on my weapon I knocked at the door, which was opened by a bright looking young man in his shirtsleeves who invited me in. As soon as the door was closed he drew a gun from his hip pocket and laid it on the table. Simultaneously I drew my revolver and put it down beside it. Mine was a .45 while his was only a .38.

"I've got you beat," I said. "What else have you got?"

Then he laughed and introduced himself as the editor of the Spokane Sunday Sun, a weekly newspaper that was then raising the devil throughout the Northwest. It was a straight-out scandal sheet, high-class but ruthless, and had been scattering sensationalism, fear and anxiety for months. But it had left Butte alone, for some reason, though it was the most promising field in the country. He said his only reason for asking me to come up unannounced was to protect me from gossip, in case we got together.

He said they had been unable to get the right correspondent in Butte, which explained why it had never figured in their columns. He had looked the camp over several times, but could not find the man they wanted, a reporter clean and honest but knowledgeable about all that went on beneath the surface. From inquiries he had made he thought I was the man he was after, and he made me a very attractive offer for a weekly letter. The whole thing was to be surrounded with secrecy, naturally. Mail was to go and come in plain envelopes, and there would be very little correspondence. No one in the world but he would know that I was the man who wrote the stuff.

"We don't want what everybody knows," he said, "but what everybody doesn't know. The stuff may be as scandalous as you like, the more scandalous it is the better. But it must be true, so that it can be defended if there is a libel suit. It is alright to say that a man is a murderer or that he beats his wife or steals money, but you must be prepared to prove it. The Sun is a scandal sheet, right enough, and it is making money hand over fist, but the way it has made it is by being ready to prove every charge we make. But we don't want any milk-and-water stuff; the daily papers handle all of that. What we want is the stuff the daily papers are afraid to touch. How about it?"

I've forgotten what he offered, but it was surprising. But that did not interest me at all. What did interest me was the chance I saw to even accounts with some men in the camp who were "dealing from the bottom" all of the time, yet who knew the Standard would never bawl them out. So I told him I would write one article and see how it went and that after that we could talk about a permanent appointment, though a regular connection with the Sun was the farthest thing from my mind. He was greatly pleased with the

Hell With the Lid Off

prospects and assured me that we would make a team that could not be beaten.

I accordingly sat down and wrote three or four columns of the spiciest stuff that ever appeared in print in any city in the land. It was all true, but there was a libel suit in every paragraph if anyone was of a mind. Names were given and locations stated and those who were aiding or abetting the slanderous proceedings were identified. Aldermen who were living with other women, while neglecting their wives, were handled without gloves. The whole story was gossipy and interesting, and in writing it I realized that I was taking my life in my hands. But I felt secure in the promise that my name would not be revealed.

Thousands of copies of the Sun with my article were sent to Butte and sold better than hot cakes. The story created a furor. Everybody who could write was suspected by someone, but strangely enough, there was less suspicion of me than of anyone else. I denounced it, of course, and especially one paragraph which seemed aimed at me, which I had inserted intentionally to throw them off the trail. There never was a story that so aroused the multitude, and it was talked of for a week—which was a long while for Butte to talk about anything. Everything went along all right for several weeks, but with the hunt still on. Then a letter came for me from the editor of the Sun, who evidently could not restrain himself. And he probably wanted more of the same kind of stuff. It was in a plain envelope, but the cancellation stamp "Spokane" stood out like a lighthouse on a clear day. The assistant postmaster, who was also harboring a grudge, took charge of it and offered it to me, with a most suspicious look. I dismissed it, with the utmost casualness.

"That's not for me," I said, after glancing at it. "I don't know anybody in Spokane."

My manner completely disarmed the assistant postmaster, and the identity of the Sun's correspondent remained an unsolved mystery.

Until now.

CHAPTER 15

JUSTICE WITH MERCY

The docket of General Charles S. Warren

"This gentleman from the Orient, it seems, had swine and said swine did not have the flavor of an apple geranium"

General Charles S. Warren was one citizen of Butte who was loved by every man, woman and child in the camp. Where the "General" came from was a mystery, but one about which there were few worries. Some thought it was given him because he was to command the fighting men of Deer Lodge, who organized to go out when Chief Joseph was supposed to be threatening that camp with his Nez Perce warriors. Others believed it was due to the fact that he had once owned a general store in that settlement.

But it probably resulted from his war experience, for there is no doubt that he knew General Ulysses S. Grant very well, though General Warren was not at all given to talk about himself in any vainglorious way. And he was just the type of man to get into any war that was handy. One day another old bullwhacker told of an incident that occurred at Gold Creek, Montana, at the driving of the golden spike on the completion of the Northern Pacific. Grant was there and was seated in the grandstand, in the sun on the north side of the track. Warren came later, and found a string of cars between him and the stand. So he ensconced himself in the shade of a tree on the South side, along with his jug of liquor.

Pretty soon the cars were moved away and Grant and Warren spied each other.

"Hey, you, what are you doing over there?" Grant bawled across the tracks.

"Hello, you old warrior. What are you doing over there, in the sun? The liquor is over here in the shade. You'd better come over," Warren yelled in reply. So, according to the old-trailblazer, Grant, crossed over to the other side, and they divided the jug, greatly to their jubilation and peace of mind.

Warren was, in fact, one of the first settlers in the young camp. He was born at Starved Rock, aka Utica, Illinois, in 1846, and at age 20 drove a bull team with a wagon train across the plains stopping first at Deer Lodge, and then at Butte. He engaged in mining and taught school as soon as there were enough people in the camp to provide the necessary children. Later he went into partnership with Lee Mantle in real estate and mining properties He was one of the incorporators of the Inter-Mountain Company, which published the evening newspaper in Butte, and finally became a promoter, which was his natural bent.

He liked to shake dice for the drinks better than anything else except, possibly, to shake money from a tenderfoot, and even then it probably would be done with a dice box. He was a smart judge of men and had an inexhaustible fund of stories, which, unfortunately, cannot be printed. He had an unfailing sense of humor and his capacity for liquor was measured only by the bottle. All of which qualities, it will be observed, made him immensely popular in the camp.

The city of Butte got off to a running start on its incorporation on June 1st, 1879. But the transition from a rough mining camp was not effected without some objections from the old bullwhackers. They contended that a mining camp was good enough for them and, therefore, good enough for anybody. But the younger element argued that the town was growing and the railroads rushing in—Union Pacific from the South and Northern Pacific from the East—and that the camp really ought to put on a few airs, for the benefit of the crowds that would follow the railroads, if for nothing else.

So the men who had blazed the trail to the ambitious camp consented to the change, with the proviso that the head of the police department should retain the old title of city marshal. And then as the capsheaf to their humor, they elected General Charles S. Warren the first police magistrate. The general was a Republican, which at that time would have barred him from any elective office. The new country was populated largely by men from Virginia and Missouri, most of whom had never seen a Republican, and what they had heard about people of that faith was not good. But Warren had lived in the camp long enough for people to get used to him; he knew something about law, he was kindly and popular, and the old-timers who whooped him into office thought it would be a fine thing to have about the only Republican in the camp sit in judgment on riotous Democrats.

And, as sometimes happened in those turbulent days, they built better than they knew. General Warren entered upon the duties of the office with a serious mien—and a cocked eye. He kept a docket, and from this he compiled an abstract, to be sent to the mayor and city council. Nearly 20 years later he gave it to me. This document tells of the cases which came before him and the manner of their disposal. It is written in ink on yellow wrapping paper, tied together with a string, and the first page sets forth his purpose, as follows:

CHARLES S. WARREN,
City Judge, Butte.

ADDENDUM
HISTORICAL, FINANCIAL AND ITEMIZED REPORT

Of the private business and Official duties of the Police Magistrate of the City of Butte, Deer Lodge County, Montana Territory for the month beginning June 2nd, 1879, and ending June 30th, 1879.

Abstract of Docket, Annotated, Revised and Enlarged for the use and benefit of the Mayor and city council of the city of Butte and all new beginners.

And respectfully submitted by the Police Magistrate as a guide to the aforesaid gentlemen.

The record sets forth the opening of the court and the highly unsatisfactory ending of the first case on the docket, as follows:

"Be it remembered that on this 2nd day of June, A.D. 1879, the Police Judge of the City of Butte arose from his couch with a lark. Having filed his official bond and swallowed the Iron Clad (oath of office) the court observed the beauties of nature as he wended his way toward the Temple of Justice, little thinking that an unfortunate was there awaiting him, and was not a little startled by observing one David Hodnett in the prisoner's box. Whereupon the court purchased a six dollar docket at his own expense and called the court to order, with the following officers of the court present:

Hon. Charles S. Warren, Police Magistrate
Hon. Geo. W. Stapleton, City Attorney
Major Josiah F. Beck, City Marshal

and proceeded to call the court to order, when the cause of

The City of Butte, Plaintiff
vs.
David Hodnett, Defendant,

was called to the notice of the court. David, it seems, had been on a drunk the previous evening and had taken occasion to make a bluff at Officer Lytle and landed in the calaboose. The court, after a full hearing of the case, fined Mr. Hodnett $25 and costs of suit. David, however, having business in Deadwood, departed from the jurisdiction of the court while out trying to rustle the funds, and the city, therefore, is loser of the $25, and the court and its officers are out and injured their fees in the first case on the docket, which, to say the least, is a trifle discouraging to the Court, Attorney and Bijah. This case is designated as Case No. 1 on the Docket of the Court."

"Shortly after David Hodnett retired the cause of

The City of Butte, Plaintiff
vs.
William Whitman, Defendant,

which is designated on the records of the Court as case No. 2, was called to the notice of the Court. It seems from the complaint and the evidence that William was giving lessons in horsemanship on the streets of Butte, all of which is contrary to the ordinances of said City. The court, thinking a reminder of a fine of $5 and costs of suit would be a great benefit to William, fined him the aforesaid amount. Paid.

"After the Court had been to breakfast the cause of

The City of Butte, Plaintiff
vs.
Susan Roe, a Chinawoman

whose real name is unknown, Defendant, came up.

This is a case of nuisance, keeping a disorderly hog pen within the limits of said city. Susan was arrested and brought into court and answers to the name of Susan. With Susan came one Davy Todd, who claimed to be the owner and guardian of Susan. But the Court having sufficient reason to believe the fair Susan guilty, assessed a fine of $25 and costs, which very much outraged Davy. The funds not being forthcoming, the Court ordered the gentle Susan to the calaboose in default of payment. Davy came into court and went security for Susan, but the Court, deeming the security insufficient, refused to take it, when Davy paid the amount, except $11, for which marquis Geo. W. Todd went security and paid.

"When the court proceeded to hear the merits of Cause No. 4,

The City of Butte, Plaintiff
vs.
John Doe, a Chinaman,

whose real name is unknown, Defendant.

This cause came under the observation of the Court on the first day's proceedings, June 2nd, 1879, and was a case of keeping an odorous hog pen. Defendant answers to the name of Ah Fun and is by the court assessed a fine of $10 and costs, which is paid.

"The Court by this time thinking a sufficiency of business had been done for the first day was reposing in his office when Marshal Beck brought in David Mathens, another unfortunate, which is designated as Case No 5.

The City of Butte, Plaintiff
vs.
David Mathens, Defendant.

Mr. Mathens, it seems, was found on the sidewalk of the city soundly wrapped in the arms of Morpheus, owing to an overdose of 'Kentucky Favorite.' The Court charged the said Mathens $10 and costs for his slumber, of which he paid $15, the fine and costs amounting to $21, leaving a balance due the City of $6 on the fine, besides the money he borrowed from the court to get out of town with. Which ended the first day's business.

"Make hay while the sun shines," says the record, after three petty cases had been disposed of, but does not seem to have been in the mind of the City Marshal, for now we go through a season of depression, and our next case, No. 9, does not appear until Wednesday, June 1st, 1879, when the case of John Pearson graces the pages of the docket. John had been on a drunk and was fined $5 and costs, which amount the Court is unable to get his hands on as John up to date has not settled.

Sam Wan was hauled into court for killing swine, contrary to ordinance. "But the Court," says the record, "after being satisfied that the killing was a part of a religious sacrifice and offering to Deity, and the Court having been told that in Holy Writ it is commanded to enlighten the heathen, and our Constitution guaranteeing him the same rights as other foreigners, the Court, feeling that justice demanded his release, ordered the cause dismissed."

One can imagine the joy with which the General made this entry on June 14th: "And now into the Temple comes a new priest of justice; E.S. Thompson, makes his first appearance as City Attorney and Assistant Dice Shaker to the Court."

The case of David Loyd quite upset the dignity of the court. Says the record:

"The docket of the court upon this case is voluminous. The defendant was arrested for an improper exposure of his person, was brought into court and after the Court had requested him to behave in a gentlemanly manner, but not heeding the remarks of the Court and being boisterous was fined $10 for contempt of court. But he, the defendant, insisting that he was the owner of the ranch and making much noise, was by the Court fined an additional amount for contempt of court. Defendant then appeared by his brother and enters a plea of guilty to the charges and is fined $1 and costs of suit, making a total of $36, which is paid."

Case No 19
The City of Butte, Plaintiff
vs.
Simon Schroedel, Defendant.

The evidence in this case leads to the belief that Simon is addicted to the use of language more forcible than polite, all of which Section No. 1 of Ordinance No. 1 forbids, for which the Court gave Simon the sum of $25 and costs. Simon was incarcerated in the city jail at the rate of $5 per day until he liquidated by labor on the streets of the City.

Case No. 20
The City of Butte, Plaintiff
vs.
Phillip Porchen, Defendant.

Mr. Porchen was arrested and brought before the Court for assault and battery upon the person of Simon Schroedel. Philip has been an old and respected citizen of Butte since the days that tried men's souls. He has contributed vast sums to the development of the mineral resources of Summit Valley Mining District and no person has appealed to him in vain for relief. But civilization with its attendant blessings (city government, etc.,) has softened the rugged features of the scene and Philip appears in court in charge of the City Marshal, robed in the garb of woe. The Court, after patiently hearing the evidence, thinks that a fine of $50 and costs would, in a measure, prolong the life of Mr. Porchen, imposes the aforesaid fine, together with costs, but relenting, remits $30 of the fine, and the balance stands to the credit of the City, subject to the drafts of its unrelenting creditors.

Case No. 21
The City of Butte, Plaintiff
vs.
J. Holmes, Defendant.

This free loving defendant is accused of using language toward a lady which would warrant any gentleman in kicking the posterior of said Defendant. The Defendant comes into court in custody of Officer Beck and after the court investigates the case, fines said Holmes $10 and costs, but afterwards remits $5 of the fine. The fine of $5 is paid.

Case No. 22
The City of Butte, Plaintiff
vs.
Mrs. Catherine Shore, Defendant.

Action commenced on the 21st day of June, 1879, against defendant for using vulgar and abusive language toward J. Holmes. The evidence shows the lady was justified in calling the plaintiff the names proved by him. And the Court by discharging the defendant feels that the end of justice is satisfied.

Case No. 23
The City of Butte, Plaintiff
vs.
Fred, a Celestial gentleman, Defendant.

whose Oriental name is to the Court unknown.

This gentleman from the Orient, it seems, had swine; that said swine did not have the flavor of an apple geranium. On the contrary it appears that said swine were obnoxious to the law abiding citizens of lower Main Street, all of which the ordinances of said City expressly forbid. Frederick was somewhat surprised that, in the 19th century, keeping swine after the devil had been cast out was against the peace and dignity of the citizens of Butte. However, the Court nominated $10 and costs as the amount for which Frederick was liable. He settled.

Case No. 24
The City of Butte, Plaintiff
vs.
John Doe, Defendant

whose Christian name, pedigree and antecedents are to the Court a matter of proof.

This action was commenced on the 24th of June, 1879, charging the defendant with a violation of the City Ordinances, by imbibing too frequently and coquetting too often, with bug juice. The defendant comes into Court and answers to the name of Daniel Dwyer, pleads guilty and is by the Court fined $5 and costs, by way of advice. Paid."

So the docket continued justice being always tempered with mercy, with both subject to the law of common sense in the light of all of the facts.

General Warren later went to New York and Ivo Bogan, assistant manager of the Ambassador Hotel in Los Angeles, ran into him at the corner of Fifth Avenue and 34th Street.

"Hello General," he said, cheerily. "What do you think of this camp?"

"It's a pretty good camp," replied Warren, with quite a patronizing air, "but it's too far from Butte to amount to much."

That was Butte of the 1890s, and for a short time thereafter it thought it was the greatest city in the world. And it was.

CREAMERY CAFE

ACKNOWLEDGEMENTS

Melissa Smith FitzGerald and I are grateful to the Butte-Silver Bow Public Archives for enabling publication of this book. The Archives, situated in a 121-year-old fire station at the base of the legendary "Richest Hill on Earth," has in its vaults and drawers vast collections that salute the history of mining, the labor movement and Western immigration

Archives Technician Kim Murphy Kohn was among the first to read Horace Smith's manuscript, buried for 80 years. She analyzed it, categorized it and alerted me to its significance and readability.

David McCumber, editor of the Montana Standard and the regional editor for Lee Enterprises newspapers across the West, brought me from Washington D.C. to Montana for a week in the winter of 2019 for the Mining City Writing Project. He also offered advice on the manuscript.

Sandra Olivetti Martin, my partner in life and in New Bay Books, partook with me of Butte's great generosity and character (albeit at a time when 6 above was a warming trend) and helped guide this manuscript through production.

Christine Martin, curator of the Clark Chateau, guided us on tours through the town and the historic chateau, where I gave my culminating reading.

Butte-based artists Toni and Paul Secomb welcomed us with the warmth of hospitality, housing us for my residency in Toni's inspiring studio in a refurbished historic dwelling on Quartz Street.

Christine Davis McDermott and Melissa Smith FitzGerald helped prepare the manuscript after it was retrieved from an upstairs trunk in FitzGeralds's Virginia home.

Some of the photos herein are part of the Butte Archives C. Owen Smithers Collection. Funding for the cataloging of this collection was provided by the National Historical Publications and Records Commission, Superfund Advisory & Redevelopment Trust Authority, Montana Cultural Trust, the Dennis and Phyllis Washington Foundation, and Montana Resources.

Friends of the Butte Archives—17 West Quartz Street, Butte MT 59701—is where to send donations to assist its valuable work.

Glossary

American Protective Association (APA). An anti-Catholic society operated briefly in the late 19th century by Protestants, particularly strong in the American Midwest. They took part in a famous Butte brawl in 1894.

Arms of Morpheus. Sound asleep; from the belief in ancient Greece that Morpheus (son of Hypnos, god of sleep) is the god of dreams.

Bullwhacker. A term from the early settlement of the West referring to the driver of an ox wagon or other heavy conveyance.

Camp. When gold and silver was discovered in the American West, miners would move in and organize a camp, establishing settlements that might evolve into boomtowns. That was the case in San Francisco in the gold rush era and in Butte in the 1860s, where a mining camp that later became Butte City drew miners from across the country and abroad.

Chuck-a-luck. A casino game played with three dice typically using an hourglass-shaped wire cage, the reason the game also was called birdcage. Bettors have five different options related to the totals of pips (black dots) before the cage is turned and the dice fall.

Copper glance. Copper sulfide, a grayish-black copper ore mineral with a metallic luster.

Faro. A card game born in 17th century France that became a favorite gambling pastime in the American frontier. A simple game with reasonable odds in which players bet against the house, putting bets on a green cloth with painted images of cards from Ace through King. Dealer drops two cards per turn from a 52-card deck and bettors wager on which cards will—or won't—come up by putting "coppers," or chips, on the painted images.

Fishplates. The forged steel plates used to bolt railroad tracks together.

Grindstone. A thick and heavy disk of stone mounted so that it will revolve to grind, sharpen or polish. In Butte, revelers would roll huge unmounted grindstones down sloping Main Street for amusement.

Heap roasting. The metallurgical process of removing sulfur from oil by heating. It uses gas–solid reactions at elevated temperatures to purifying the ore. As might be expected, heap roasting has been a significant source of air pollution.

Latchstring. A cord on a latch that may be left hanging outside the door to permit the raising of the latch from the outside or drawn inside to prevent intrusion.

Oil floatation process. A method in mineral processing starting in the 1890s to separate and concentrate ores.

Orangeman. A member of the Orange Order, a Protestant sectarian organization founded in Ireland and Scotland. Adherents march on July 12 to commemorate the victory of William of Orange at the Battle of the Boyne in 1690.

Rabble-heads. Elongated hunks of iron, narrow, but sometimes a half-foot long, for use atop skimming tools used in smelting.

Sluff. A game of cards typically played for drinks rather than money that became the rage in the West late in the 19th century. A rather simple game of trick-taking played with a 36-card deck, deuce through five removed, notable for odd phraseology. A player may "frog," "have his dink," and often, these words are said: "Now, damn you sluff."

Soda to hock. Beginning to end, for the first and last cards in a game of Faro.

Sonnykabick. An disparaging term in place of its sound-alike epithet deployed frequently by Smith at a time when profanity seldom reached news columns.

Vigilantes. People bent on justice in the 1860s when the region was part of the Idaho Territory and law enforcement and courts had scant authority in remote mining camps. Initially modeled after the San Francisco Committee on Vigilance, Montana committees used hanging and other methods to deal with cattle rustling, horse thievery and various crimes—until civil justice reached the territory.

Photo Credits

Page vi

Panoramic view of Butte, Montana at the dawn of the 20th century when its richness and vitality was scarcely surpassed. Its population of 60,000 was more than twice that of Butte proper today.

Library of Congress "Copyright 1904 by H. Wellge." Milwaukee: H. Wellge, Milwaukee, Wis., Publisher, [1904] © 1904 Library of Congress Geography and Map Division Washington, D.C. 20540-4650.

Page viii

A cross-cut photo of Butte more than a century ago with its mining operations in the shadow of the Rocky Mountains. Butte copper and ores helped propel the nation into an era when people would be wired together with electricity and telephones.

Library of Congress B.E._view,_Butte,_Montana_LCCN2007662443, Todd Photographic Co., c1914. J195797 U.S. Copyright Office, September 5, 1914; DLC/PP-1914:44837. — On front: "Exposition series #4154."

Page x

Street scene of Butte during Smith's time featuring the Hoffman Hotel and Restaurant on East Park St., which claimed the city's largest dining room open around the clock and a private entrance leading to private dining rooms.

Montana Historical Society

Page xvii

Late 19th Century Newspaper Ad.

Newspapers.com

Page xviii

Undated photo of Horace Herbert Smith.

Melissa Smith FitzGerald

P.16-17

Bar scene: A teetotaler, Smith was viewed as an oddball in a town where saloons never closed. "Everybody gambled and everybody drank and everybody enjoyed life to the full," he wrote.

Montana Standard

Page 34

Presbyterian minister Rev. E.J. Groeneveld, of the First Presbyterian Church. The Rev. E.J. Groeneveld of the First Presbyterian Church became the toast of Butte after going head-to-head with a despised atheist in a Sunday competition that captivated people from every strata of life. The stunt, scripted by Horace Smith and his newspaper, helped to build a new church and propelled Groeneveld's career in the pulpit.

Retouched photo derived from *The Pioneer work of the Presbyterian Church in Montana*, page 116, edited by Rev. George Edwards.

Page 50

"Famous Anaconda Hill" photo.
Anaconda Hill, known far as "the richest hill on earth" for the ores it produced and its hilly streets that invited curious games of nighttime street revelry.

Butte-Silver Bow Public Library

Page 68

Nothing needed to make the Anaconda Standard a great paper was overlooked, and Marcus Daly's newspaper claimed to be the best from St. Paul to San Francisco. The copper king recruited smart journalists from the East, signed up the Associated Press and had a wire strung over the 20 miles from the newsroom in Anaconda to the Butte bureau where Horace Smith worked, Standard operators situated at each end.

Newspapers.com

Page 76

Marcus Daly, an Irish immigrant, was the much beloved in his time "copper king" who discovered the enormous copper vein that wired America and enabled his racehorses, mansions and vast wealth. His Montana holdings were valued at $75 million at the time of his death, in 1900.

Montana Standard

Page 82

Headframe, Photo 11.098.02.

C. Owen Smithers Photograph Collection, 2014.204, Butte-Silver Bow Public Archives, Montana.

Page 90

Political cartoon from the 28 October 1900 issue of The Anaconda Standard (Montana) depicting the multimillionaire William A. Clark bribing state legislators to vote for him to become the United States Senator from Montana. Clark is throwing wads of money through hotel transom windows.

Newspapers.com

Page 96

Broadway Crowd at Night, Photo 30.003.02-.03.

C. Owen Smithers Photograph Collection, 2014.204, Butte-Silver Bow Public Archives, Butte, Montana.

Page 108

Turn of the century Butte, Montana Jail.

Photo from TripAdvisor:
https://www.tripadvisor.com/LocationPhotoDirectLink-g45106-d3184365-i146091008-Old_Butte_Historical_Adventures-Butte_Montana.html

Hell With the Lid Off

Page 122

Anaconda Standard front on Jan. 16, 1895, the morning after the Kenyon-Connell warehouse explosions from illegally stored dynamite. Horace Smith, who escaped injury rushing to the scene after the first blast, writes that his coverage may have been the best straight-news reporting of his career.

Newspapers.com

Page 127

Devastation from the dynamite explosions was profound, and the official death toll was 62 in what would be known as the Great Disaster of 1895. All but three members of the Butte Fire Department died.

Kenyon Connell Warehouse Explosions. PH 106.

Kenyon-Connell Company Explosion Photograph Collection. Butte Silver-Bow Public Archives.

Page 132

A copper king and financier, mining engineer Fritz Augustus Heinze arrived in Butte from Brooklyn in 1889 and deployed his brains and guile to become one of the region's three copper kings, later to become a financier in New York steeped in controversy. Smith, in New York during Heinze's troubles, writes vividly of the collapse of the hard-drinking Heinze, who died from liver disease at age 44.

Photograph of F. Augustus Heinze (1869-1914) "Copper King" of Butte, Montana.

Unknown Author – The Technical World Magazine 1904. Wikipedia.

Page 145

The vibrant Owsley Block in Butte around 1892, the year Horace Smith arrived. Builder Michael Owsley was a Missouri native who made his fortune in the livery business during the mining boom and became a mayor of Butte.

Butte-Silver Bow Public Library

Page 146

An Independence Day riot erupted after an anti-Catholic banner from the short-lived American Protection Association unfurled in a downtown saloon. The melee claimed the life of a Butte police officer; no one ever was convicted in the shooting. Horace Smith offers details from his vantage point and writes that preparing to plunge into the crowd, he diverted to a nearby shop to secure a box of .45 caliber shells for his gun.

American Protective Association riot, Butte, Montana, July 4, 1894, Photo 47.046.01.

C. Owen Smithers Photograph Collection, 2014.204. Butte-Silver Bow Public Archives, Butte, Montana.

Page 162

Trainers from the East brought horses to Butte's tracks to compete for big purses in races that, for a period, weren't always on the up-and-up. Smith describes big crowds and furious betting, "and a large part of it was done by women, good and bad alike." Pictured at the iconic Round Barn near Twin Bridges, Montana, is the horse Spokane (left), the only Montana horse to win the Kentucky Derby (1889).

Noah Armstrong's Horse Spokane near Twin Bridges, Photo 20.041.01.

C. Owens Smithers Photograph Collection, 2014.204, Butte-Silver Bow Public Archives, Butte, Montana.

Page 171

Butte's club football team would travel to face foes in California and the Northwest, and Horace Smith, whose beat included sports, accompanied them. He writes about the Montana team's particularly rough style of play. "When the other team started it, the Butte team always finished it."

Newspapers.com

Pages 174-175

Long after leaving Butte, Smith edited the book *Roosevelt in the Rough*, accounts of the 26th president's hunting and adventures over the years with noted Montana outdoorsman Jack Willis. Passages that triggered controversy in the day described the president's wild joy ride after a rowdy dinner in Butte in 1903.

Theodore Roosevelt Visits Butte, Montana. Photo 32.056.04.

C. Owen Smithers Photograph Collection, 2014.204. Butte-Silver Bow Public Archives, Butte, Montana.

Page 188

Charles S. Warren

Illinois-born Charles S. Warren was a Union Army soldier who drove a bull train to the Montana Territory shortly after the Civil War. He established a mining company while pursuing real estate ventures and became a police magistrate in Butte.

Montana Standard

P. 192

Charles Warren cartoon.

Montana Standard

P. 208

Broadway Crowd at Night, Photo 30.003.02-.03.

C. Owen Smithers Photograph Collection, 2014.204, Butte-Silver Bow Public Archives, Butte, Montana.

Page 209

Horace "Bert" Smith in a 1910 photo with his wife, Annie White Fleming, and infant son, Horace Herbert Smith Jr., taken in New York City, where Smith settled after his years in Butte. The child was born in a New York hospital above a box of Virginia dirt, a demand by Smith's proud Virginian wife. The couple lived apart for years. Smith died in Virginia in 1936.

Melissa Smith FitzGerald

www.ingramcontent.com/pod-product-compliance
Lightning Source LLC
Chambersburg PA
CBHW020525080526
44583CB00013B/743